LANGUAGE ACQUISITION & LANGUAGE DISORDERS

Volume 1

Lydia White

Universal Grammar and Second Language Acquisition

UNIVERSAL GRAMMAR
AND
SECOND LANGUAGE ACQUISITION

by

LYDIA WHITE
McGill University

JOHN BENJAMINS PUBLISHING COMPANY
AMSTERDAM/PHILADELPHIA

1989

Library of Congress Cataloging-in-Publication Data

White, Lydia.
  Universal Grammar and second language acquisition / by Lydia White.
    p.   cm. -- (Language acquisition and language disorders; v. 1)
Includes bibliographical references.
Includes index.
1. Second language acquisition. 2. Language acquisition. 3. Grammar, Comparative and
general. I. Title. II. Series.
P118.2.W4   1989
401'.93 -- dc20   89-48055
ISBN 90 272 2461 7 (hb) / 90 272 2462 5 (pb) (Eur., alk. paper)   CIP
ISBN 1-55619-092-1 (hb) / 1-55619-093-X (pb) (US, alk. paper)

Table of Contents

Preface

In this book, the potential relationship between linguistic universals and second language acquisition will be explored. In particular, we shall be concerned with a principles and parameters approach to Universal Grammar (UG), as realized in Government and Binding (GB) Theory (Chomsky 1981a). This theory assumes that principles and parameters of UG constitute an innately given body of knowledge which constrains first language (L1) acquisition.

Assuming the correctness of this general approach, the question arises as to whether UG remains available in non-primary language acquisition. This has recently become an area of considerable interest in second language (L2) acquisition research, with a variety of different opinions being represented, ranging from researchers who consider that UG plays no role in (adult) second language acquisition, to the opposite extreme of those who consider that it operates exactly as it does in L1 acquisition. There are also a variety of positions somewhere in the middle, which assume that UG operates but not as effectively as in L1 acquisition, due to the intervention of other factors. These different positions will be reviewed, consideration being given both to theoretical argumentation, and to data (experimental and otherwise) which are used to support the various positions.

There is a growing literature in this area. Not surprisingly, papers reporting on current research have to take many issues for granted, and they often address several different topics at once. In discussing current research, I will often focus only on those aspects that fit with the general themes of this book. In many cases, I have reported only selected aspects of experimental results, in an attempt to present the more central issues. Readers are encouraged to go to the original sources for further details and discussion, especially if they are themselves intending to pursue experimental research in this area. I should also make it clear that, as this is a rapidly developing area, researchers are constantly revising their hypotheses, and the positions discussed in this book do not necessarily represent views currently held by those cited.

The book is organized as follows. Chapter 1 outlines arguments for UG in L1 acquisition, and presents a brief overview of GB theory; Chapter 2 discusses why these arguments should be extended to L2 acquisition. Chapter 3 reviews research on principles of UG in L2 acquisition and Chapter 4 looks at the role of parameters. Chapter 5 considers the effects of markedness, as defined within the UG perspective. Chapter 6 looks at the relevance of learnability theories for L2 acquisition. Chapter 7 discusses the implications of cognitive modularity. No knowledge of generative grammar is presupposed.

Special thanks are due to Kevin Gregg and Peter Skehan for their very pertinent and detailed comments on the manuscript. I should like also like to thank the following people for their helpful comments on the manuscript as a whole, or on individual chapters: Mark Baker, Robert Bley-Vroman, Harald Clahsen, Lynn Eubank, Makiko Hirakawa, Eric Kellerman, Juana Liceras, Irene Mazurkewich, Bill Rutherford, Jackie Schachter.

This research was conducted with the assistance of a Canada Research Fellowship, #455-87-0201, from the Social Sciences and Humanities Research Council of Canada, for which I am grateful.

1 Linguistic theory and language acquisition

1.1 Introduction

In this book, potential relationships between linguistic theory and second language acquisition will be explored. We shall adopt a framework that considers the following three questions to be of fundamental concern (Chomsky 1981b, 1986):

    i. What constitutes knowledge of language?
    ii. How is such knowledge acquired?
    iii. How is such knowledge put to use?

In asking these questions, Chomsky is concerned with adult native speaker knowledge and use of language, and with child first language acquisition only. An aim of this book is to suggest that if these questions are posed about second language knowledge and second language acquisition, the same answers that current linguistic theory offers for first language knowledge and acquisition may prove to be relevant. In particular, we shall focus on Chomsky's answer to the second question, and explore the extent to which his answer holds for non-primary language acquisition.

1.2 Knowledge of language

Knowledge of language, technically known as linguistic *competence*, is assumed to be represented in the form of a generative grammar, an abstract system of principles and rules which produce the grammatical sentences of a language. Principles and rules account for such formal properties of language as syntax, phonology, morphology, and certain aspects of semantics.

The knowledge which is represented in this way is unconscious knowledge; most people are not aware of the systematic nature of their language and cannot articulate the rules and principles that they in fact follow. The system of knowledge is also very rich: as well as being able to understand and produce utterances which they have never heard before, adults and children know that certain utterances are grammatical, others ungrammatical, that some sentences have more than one meaning (are ambiguous), that some meanings can be represented by more than one sentence (paraphrases). None of this knowledge appears to be taught.

The grammar representing one's unconscious linguistic knowledge is a mental construct — it is psychologically real — and it underlies language use. Linguists working within this framework may (and do) disagree about the precise form that a grammar should take but they agree that what they are trying to discover is the way in which language is mentally represented.

Let us look at some examples of knowledge of English which we possess if we are native speakers, knowledge which is rule-governed but which is, in most cases, quite unconscious. We are not concerned here (or elsewhere in the book) with the precise formalisms that linguists adopt to characterize rules and principles.

Unconscious phonological knowledge will serve as a first example. Consider plural formation in spoken English. Pronunciation of the plural varies: the plural forms of the words *back*, *cap* and *cat* are pronounced differently from those of *bag*, *cab* and *cad*. The former are all pluralized by the addition of an [s] sound, whereas the latter get a [z]. This is something completely regular and rule-governed. If English is your mother tongue, you may not be able to tell someone else when and why you use one pronunciation rather than the other but you will unconsciously know which sound is appropriate. Given nonsense words like *gluck* and *glub*, native speakers will pluralize the former with [s] and the latter with [z]. Our linguistic behaviour here can be explained on the assumption that our competence includes a phonological rule which, informally and omitting many details, specifies that word-final voiced sounds must be followed by a voiced version of the plural morpheme, while voiceless sounds get the voiceless form.

Another example of rule-governed but usually unconscious knowledge is provided by the suffix *-able*, which attaches to verbs to form adjectives, such as *readable*, *washable*, *breakable*, *usable*, *debatable*, etc. This way of forming adjectives is quite productive and can be applied to new verbs that enter the language, e.g. *xeroxable, faxable*. However, native speakers also unconsciously know that there are cases where *-able* cannot be added to a verb to form an adjective: **dieable, *goable, *sleepable, *sitable, *weepable*, etc, are not possible.[1] These nonexistent forms are not simply excluded on grounds of meaning, since a sentence like *This bed is sleepable* would make sense. Our competence not only includes a rule of *-able* attachment but also the knowledge that this rule of adjective formation is (on the whole) limited to transitive verbs.

Finally, we can consider an example from syntax. We 'know' that in cases like (1) and (3) there are two possible forms of the sentence, whereas in (2) and (4) there are not, even though an apparently identical sequence of words (*look up* and *turn down*) is used:

(1) a. John looked up the telephone number
    b. John looked the telephone number up
(2) a. John looked up the hill
    b. *John looked the hill up
(3) a. Mary turned down my idea
    b. Mary turned my idea down
(4) a. Mary turned down the street
    b. *Mary turned the street down

Our knowledge of English includes the fact that certain forms like *up* and *down* may have different functions in different sentences, in the above cases either as prepositions or as particles. Only when a particle is present is there a choice as to its position.

The above are some over-simplified examples of unconscious knowledge which is systematic and rule-governed. We shall see later that our linguistic competence consists of much more than this; the major focus of current linguistic theory is to try to account for language in terms of abstract principles, rather than language-specific rules. These principles are assumed to be universal, the emphasis being on what languages have in common at some underlying level.

Chomsky's question: *What constitutes knowledge of language?* is directed towards the knowledge possessed by adults. His second question concerns the problem of how children come by this knowledge. Chomsky argues that the acquisition of a grammar is only possible if it is guided by some kind of innate structure, specifically linguistic in nature, usually called Universal Grammar (UG). In other words, not all knowledge of language in fact has to be acquired, because some of it is already 'built in'. A central goal of linguistic theory is to come up with a characterization of UG, of the principles that shape our linguistic knowledge.

1.3 The language acquisition task and the language acquisition problem

Certain assumptions about first language (L1) acquisition are fundamental to generative grammar and have led to the proposal that innate linguistic principles must be involved. The acquisition task can be schematized as follows:[2]

(5)

Input ⟶ Grammar

On the basis of linguistic input, children must arrive at an internalized system, a grammar, which will allow them to understand language produced by others and to produce language themselves, and which will constitute their knowledge of language.

The problem is that the linguistic competence of adults is extremely intricate, complex and subtle. All (normal) children acquire this linguistic competence, which extends beyond the primary input (the kind of language which children are exposed to) in various ways. Children and adults can understand and produce sentences which they have never heard before. Apart from dialectal differences, the competence of adult native speakers of the same language is essentially similar; that is, adults achieve the same end result (a complex competence grammar), even though their exposure to data in the course of acquisition may have been quite different — they may have heard different input, or the same input in different orders, or they may not have been exposed to certain kinds of input at all.

Linguists motivate UG by pointing to the end result of language acquisition, namely the adult grammar in all its complexity, arguing that there is no way this could be acquired without prior knowledge of some kind, given the kind of input that children are exposed to in the course of acquisition. In particular, three problems with the input are often discussed: (i) input underdetermines the final grammar, (ii) it is often degenerate, (iii) it does not contain negative evidence. For such reasons, language acquisition is often described in terms of a *projection* problem, or a *logical* problem, or a *learnability* problem; that is, there is a mismatch between the primary linguistic input and the system actually attained. The proposed solution to this problem is that the acquisition of a grammar must be mediated by Universal Grammar. Thus, the model in (5) will be amended as follows:

(6)

Input ⟶ UG ⟶ Grammar

Universal Grammar consists of principles which constrain the form and functioning of grammars. It gives the child advance knowledge of many abstract and complex properties of language, so that these do not have to be learned solely on the basis of linguistic input or by means of general learning strategies. In language acquisition, then, there is an interaction between the innate UG and the linguistic input from the language being acquired.

1.4 Three problems with input

It is important to understand that the projection problem is a genuine problem. In the following sections, we shall consider the three problems with the input in more detail. The first problem (underdetermination) is by far the most serious one, providing the best motivation for innate, specifically linguistic structure. A number of researchers have recently tried to argue that the second (degeneracy) and third (no negative evidence) problems do not in fact arise, and hence that one can dismiss the need for a concept like UG. However, these attempts are misconceived, and stem from a misunderstanding of the main issues.

1.4.1 *Underdetermination*

A number of aspects of language are *underdetermined* by the input. That is, the linguistic competence of children and adults includes properties which are not immediately obvious and which are not explicitly taught; the grammar that underlies our language use, which has to be acquired by children, goes far beyond the actual sentences that an individual learner may happen to have been exposed to.

Here we will touch on a few examples of linguistic knowledge that goes beyond the input. In all these examples, an acquisition problem arises if we impute to the child only some general cognitive ability to make analogies or generalizations solely on the basis of input. If learning were of this type, one would expect the child to make many false generalizations, to produce errors which have not been attested in child language, and to fail to work out certain properties of the language.

1.4.1.1 *Wanna-contraction*

One example is a rule in informal spoken English which allows the sequence *want to* to contract to *wanna*.[3] This can be seen in cases such as :

(7)	a.	I want to go
	b.	I wanna go
(8)	a.	John wants to go but we don't want to
	b.	John wants to go but we don't wanna
(9)	a.	Do you want to look at the chickens?
	b.	Do you wanna look at the chickens?
(10)	a.	Who do you want to see?
	b.	Who do you wanna see?

In addition to knowing the contraction possibilities like those above, adults also unconsciously know when contraction is not possible (i.e. when it leads to ungrammatical results). In (11) and (12), *want to* cannot be contracted to *wanna*:

(11)	a.	Who do you want to feed the dog?
	b.	*Who do you wanna feed the dog?
(12)	a.	Who do you want to win the race?
	b.	*Who do you wanna win the race?

In other cases still, the uncontracted sentence is ambiguous but the *wanna* form is not, as can be seen in (13). Again this is something that is part of our unconscious knowledge:

(13)	a.	Teddy is the man (who) I want to succeed
	b.	Teddy is the man (who) I wanna succeed

In (13a), one interpretation of the sentence is that *I want to succeed Teddy* and the other is that *I want Teddy to succeed (at something)*. In (13b), only the former interpretation is possible.

If the child were simply extracting generalizations from the language he or she is exposed to, it would be very difficult to arrive at correct knowledge of the distribution and interpretation of *wanna*: one would expect false analogies to be made on the basis of superficial similarities. There is nothing obvious in the input which would indicate that contraction is permissible in sentences like (7) to (10) but not in sentences like (11) and (12) or that (13b) is unambiguous whereas (13a) is ambiguous.

The acquisition of *wanna* can be explained by means of principles of UG. *Wh*-questions are derived by movement of the *wh*-word from an underlying position to the front of the sentence. An empty category (or trace *t*) marks the position from which the *wh*-question word has moved. (This proposal accounts for a wide range of syntactic phenomena and was not made specifically to deal with the *wanna* phenomenon.) In sentences like (10a), the *wh*-object has been moved, leaving a coindexed trace marking its original position, as in (14):

(14)   Who$_i$ do you want to see t$_i$?

In sentences like (11a), the *wh*-subject of the infinitive has been moved, giving a structure like (15):

(15)   Who$_i$ do you want t$_i$ to feed the dog?

Wanna-contraction is sensitive to the presence of *wh*-traces. If a trace intervenes between *want* and *to*, contraction is impossible. This explains why sentences like (11b) are ungrammatical. In the cases of grammatical contraction, there is no trace intervening between *want* and *to*. Similarly, the lack of ambiguity of (13b) is accounted for: only the interpretation where the trace does not intervene between *want* and *to* is available for contraction.

None of this information is obviously present in the input, since traces are an abstraction. The fact that *wh*-movement leaves a trace and that this trace blocks the operation of certain rules is knowledge derived from UG, and not from the input alone, or from any general non-linguistic cognitive principles.

1.4.1.2 *The distribution of complementizers*
Another example of linguistic knowledge which goes beyond the input comes from the distribution of the complementizer *that* in English. *That* is optional in a variety of structures, as can be seen in (16) to (18):

(16)   a.   I think that John is a fool
         b.   I think John is a fool

(17) a.   The girl that I met yesterday was very tall
      b.   The girl I met yesterday was very tall
(18) a.   Who do you think that Mary met yesterday?
      b.   Who do you think Mary met yesterday?

However, there are certain cases where deletion of the complementizer is obligatory, rather than optional, as in (19):

(19) a.   Who do you think arrived yesterday?
      b.   *Who do you think that arrived yesterday?

When the subject of a lower clause is moved out of its clause to the front of the sentence, *that* cannot be retained. This contrasts with extraction of objects, as in (18), where the presence of *that* is optional.

The acquisition problem is as follows: suppose that the child works out on the basis of data such as (16) to (18) that the occurrence of the complementizer is optional in English. How is the curious restriction on the complementizer in (19) discovered? Again, the assumption in generative grammar is that the distribution of the complementizer, that is, both its optional occurrence in (16) to (18) and its obligatory absence in (19), falls out from a principle of UG, the Empty Category Principle (ECP), which also accounts for a wide range of other phenomena in many different languages, as well as English. If knowledge of this principle is built in, the child does not have to induce the distribution of complementizers from the input alone. (See 1.8.2.8 for further details on this principle.)

1.4.1.3 *Constraints on* wh-*movement*
Wh-movement provides another example of knowledge going beyond input. We have already seen that *wh*-phrases can be moved to the front of the sentence to form questions. This is true for both simple and complex sentences:

(20) a.   What did John see _?
      b.   What did Mary believe that John saw _?
      c.   What did Jane say that Mary believed that John saw _?

Although *wh*-movement is very productive, there are restrictions on it. The questions in (21a) and (21d) are ungrammatical, even though the equivalent declarative sentences in (21b) and (21e) are grammatical. The ungrammaticality of (21a) and (21d) cannot be due to semantic or pragmatic factors, since (21c) and (21f), with very similar meanings, are grammatical:

(21) a. *What did Mary wonder whether John had bought?
     b. Mary wondered whether John had bought a present
     c. What did Mary hope that John had bought?
     d. *What does Mary believe the claim that John saw?
     e. Mary believes the claim that John saw a ghost
     f. What does Mary believe that John claimed to have seen?

How does the child discover that questions like (21a) and (21d) are ungrammatical? Again, the input data do not tell the child that such sentences are impossible; they are simply non-occurring. Other very similar questions, like (21c) and (21f), might be encountered. If children were extracting generalizations from the input, one would expect them to be misled by the possibility of sentences like (20), (21c) or (21f) into thinking that sentences like (21a) and (21d) are also possible.

Once again, the assumption in linguistic theory is that such restrictions on *wh*-movement do not have to be learned; they are the consequence of a principle of UG, known as Subjacency, which places certain conditions on syntactic movement. (See 1.8.2.4 for further details.)

1.4.1.4 *Pronouns*

Another area of considerable complexity is the distribution of reflexive pronouns. These require an antecedent within the same sentence, that is, a noun phrase with which they are coreferential. There are structural conditions on when coreference can and cannot occur. To illustrate the problem, we will consider the coreference possibilities only between the italicized phrases in the sentences in (22):

(22) a. *John* saw *himself*
     b. **Himself* saw *John*
     c. Looking after *himself* bores *John*
     d. **John* said that Fred liked *himself*
     e. John said that *Fred* liked *himself*
     f. *John* told *Bill* to wash *himself*
     g. *John* promised Bill to wash *himself*
     h. **John* believes that *himself* is intelligent
     i. *John* believes *himself* to be intelligent
     j. *John* showed *Bill* a picture of *himself*

Children have to discover that the reflexive pronoun usually must follow the antecedent (22a and 22b) but that this is not always so (22c); that the reflexive usually must be in the same clause as the antecedent (22a, d, e) but not always so (22f); that the reflexive can be in subject position of a non-finite embedded clause (22i) but not a finite one (22h); that the closest NP is usually the antecedent (22d, e,f) but not always so (22g); that in some cases, there is more than one possible antecedent (j) but not always so (22d,e,f,g). It would seem impossible to work out the distribution of anaphoric pronouns on a trial and error basis without a great many mistakes.

Ordinary pronouns also raise acquisition problems. As can be seen in (23), a nounphrase and a pronoun cannot refer to the same person in a simple sentence:

(23) a.   *Mary* washed *her*
      b.   *She* washed *Mary*

The situation is different in a complex sentence, as can be seen in (24):

(24) a.   *Mary* watched television before *she* had her dinner
      b.   Before *Mary* had her dinner *she* watched television
      c.   Before *she* had her dinner *Mary* watched television
      d.   *She* watched television before *Mary* had her dinner

In (24a), (24b) and (24c), *Mary* and the pronoun *she* can be coreferential. In (24d) they cannot be. How does the child work out when a pronoun may refer to someone mentioned in the same sentence and when it may not? It is not simply a matter of sentence type, since (23b) and (24d) are both ungrammatical. Nor is it a matter of linear relationships between the nounphrase and the pronoun, since Mary precedes the pronoun in (24a) and (24b) but follows it in (24c). The distribution of pronouns and reflexives (and also other anaphors and referring expressions) is a consequence of the Binding Theory, which is part of UG and hence available to guide acquisition. (This is discussed further in 1.8.2.7.) The distribution of the anaphors, pronouns and NPs is built in and does not have to be learned.

1.4.1.5 *Parasitic gaps*

Our final example is a phenomenon which is relatively rare, but which has attracted a good deal of interest in the linguistic literature recently, namely sentences with so-called *parasitic gaps*. This structure is quite marginal, and not all dialects of English accept it. Arguably, many people will never be exposed to this structure in the input at all. The importance of this example is that there are clear differences in acceptability in sentences with parasitic gaps, differences which cannot be attributed to the input, given the rarity of the structure. A parasitic gap construction has two gaps related to one earlier phrase; the second, parasitic, gap is 'licensed' by a trace in the sentence. Consider the sentences in (25):

(25) a.   John filed the letter without reading it
      b.   *John filed the letter without reading _
      c.   Which letter did John file t without reading _?
      d.   The letter which I filed t without reading _ was very long
      e.   *The letter was filed t without Bill reading _
      f.   *Who t filed the letter without Mary reminding _?

In (25a), we have a grammatical sentence with no gap, which contrasts with (25b), where the direct object is missing but there is no other earlier trace to licence it.[4] (25c) and (25d) are acceptable for speakers of dialects which allow parasitic gaps; in these sentences the missing object of *reading* is licensed by the earlier trace. In contrast, (25e) and (25f) are ungrammatical, even though there is an earlier trace in both sentences. This difference in grammaticality is unexpected if our knowledge of language derives only from analogies made on the basis of surface similarities. One does not, however, want to have to propose separate principles of UG in order to explain such a marginal construction. This is not the place to go into a detailed analysis of parasitic gaps (see the references at the end of this chapter for details), but the point is that the grammaticality of (25c) and (25d) and the ungrammaticality of (25e) and (25f) fall out from principles of UG which have been proposed to account for much more central phenomena, and which account for these as a by-product, so to speak.

To summarize the issue of underdetermination, we have seen a number of examples where the input might be expected to mislead the child into making false generalizations about the language being learned, or where it might fail to allow the child to work out various subtle phenomena. The last example consists of a case where our competence includes knowledge that may have been arrived at on the basis of little or no input at all. Many other examples of underdetermination can be found in the references at the end of this chapter. Despite the problem of underdetermination, children arrive at the full complexity of adult knowledge with comparatively little difficulty, and without the range of errors that one might anticipate, suggesting that there must be certain innate restrictions, in the form of linguistic principles, that mediate the child's acquisition of language.

1.4.2 *Degeneracy*

Another alleged problem with the input is that the language that the child hears is not always perfect. Adults make mistakes, hesitate, change their minds about what they are going to say, etc. This kind of input, that is, input which includes ungrammatical or partial forms as well as fully grammatical ones, is sometimes referred to as *degenerate*. It is potentially problematic because a language learner has no way of knowing which aspects of the input are examples of grammatical sentences and which are not, so that this could make the extracting of generalizations extremely difficult. The existence of degenerate data has constituted another argument for UG; if children have built-in knowledge of what a grammar must be like, then the presence of degenerate data will not mislead them into false hypotheses because they will know in advance that certain kinds of analyses are ruled out.

In recent years, work in developmental psycholinguistics has concentrated on properties of the input to young children and it has been shown that this input is in fact very rarely degenerate (e.g. papers in Snow and Ferguson 1977). Adults talking to young children tend to use short sentences or phrases, which constitute fully grammatical units. For this reason, it has been claimed that there is no need to postulate so much innate linguistic structure after all (Brown 1977).

This latter claim arises from a serious misconception of the main issue. The fact that input to young children is not degenerate does not remove the acquisition problem altogether. The only aspect of the problem that it removes is the confusion that could result from a mixture of ungrammatical input with grammatical input. The problem of underdetermination, as discussed above, still remains. Even totally grammatical input will underdetermine adult knowledge.

Furthermore, grammatical input in the simplified form in which it occurs when adults talk to young children will, if anything, underdetermine the adult grammar even more than non-simplified input. Simplified input fails to exemplify all sorts of complex properties of language, making the acquisition problem worse rather than better (see Wexler and Culicover 1980 for further discussion). It is not the case that properties of complex sentences are simply the sum of properties of simple sentences, so that even if children are 'helped' initially by special non-degenerate and simplified forms of input, this puts off, but does not solve, the acquisition problem.

Thus, even if one recognizes the correctness of the claim that input to young children is not degenerate, this in no way reduces the need to assume the existence of innate principles underlying language acquisition.

1.4.3 *Negative evidence*

The third problem with the input has to do with how children learn about ungrammaticality, about what sentences are **not** possible in the language they are learning. Adult linguistic competence includes unconscious knowledge of ungrammaticality as well as grammaticality. The question is: how is this achieved, how do children find out that certain things are impossible?

Let us illustrate the problem by reconsidering the case of *wh*-movement. We have seen that adults unconsciously know that sentences like (26a) are grammatical whereas sentences like (26b) are ungrammatical:

(26)   a.   What did Mary believe that John bought _?
       b.   *What did Mary believe the story that John bought _?

How do children discover that (26b) is unacceptable? Perhaps they make mistakes like (26b) and are subsequently corrected, i.e., they are explicitly informed that such sentences are not grammatical.

Evidence of this kind, that is, evidence about ungrammaticality, is known as *negative evidence*; this contrasts with *positive evidence*, which is evidence as to what is possible in a language. In the case of L1 acquisition, positive evidence consists of the utterances that the child hears (and takes note of). One possibility, then, is that knowledge of ungrammaticality is the result of negative evidence. This depends on two assumptions: (i) children get negative evidence, and (ii) children make the relevant kinds of errors. Both of these assumptions appear to be incorrect.

For negative input to be an effective means of learning, one must be able to guarantee that children get it and use it. Research on L1 acquisition suggests that children usually do not get corrected when they make mistakes of grammatical form (Brown and Hanlon 1970) and where they are corrected, they ignore it (Braine 1971). Nor do children solicit evidence about structure. Thus, this means of eliminating incorrect hypotheses is not reliably available.

The unavailability of negative evidence in L1 acquisition has recently been questioned (e.g. Hirsh-Pasek et al. 1984; Bohannon and Stanowicz 1988), resulting in misconceptions similar to those discussed in 1.4.2 above.

It has been suggested that negative evidence is in fact available in first language acquisition, and hence that this reduces the need for an innate component. However, there are various problems with the kind of negative evidence that has been reported. It is often vague and its occurrence is unreliable. Hirsh-Pasek et al. (1984) show that mothers repeat (and in the process correct) young children's ungrammatical forms more often than their grammatical ones. The problem is that mothers also repeat and rephrase grammatical utterances as well. The child, therefore, cannot know for any particular repetition whether or not it signals that the child's utterance had been incorrect. In addition, Hirsh-Pasek et al. found that such repetitions were most frequent with very young children; they stopped long before the course of language acquisition was completed. Bohannon and Stanowicz (1988) show that there is a significant difference between the type of feedback given to ungrammatical utterances (where parents do things like giving grammatical rephrasings of the utterance) and grammatical utterances (where parents give verbatim repetitions). However, the majority of utterances received no rephrasings or repetitions at all. Furthermore, the kinds of errors that parents responded to were not at all the kinds of thing that principles of UG are concerned with.

These attempts to show that children do, after all, have access to negative input, that parents respond differentially to errors, miss an essential point: if certain errors never occur, parents cannot respond differentially to them. Negative evidence is irrelevant in the absence of certain kinds of errors. It turns out that there are many logically possible errors which children never make. For example, children do not assume that ungrammatical forms of *wh*-movement are possible (Otsu 1981). While children do produce forms which are incorrect from the adult's point of view, the errors that they make are far more limited in type than might be expected.

Plausible theories of language acquisition must assume realistic input, in other words, that children proceed largely on the basis of positive evidence, and must explain how children come by their unconscious knowledge of language on the basis of this kind of input, without making certain types of errors. The assumption in generative grammar is that certain hypotheses about language are never entertained by the child in the first place, that knowledge about what is not possible stems from UG. Indeed, much of UG consists of negative constraints, principles which provide information about what languages may not do. This built-in knowledge in some sense compensates for the lack of availability of negative input. For example, *Subjacency* places certain limitations on *wh*-movement (see 1.8.2.4 for details), both removing any need for negative evidence about sentences like (26b) — the child already knows the constraints on movement — and explaining why errors like (26b) are not made in the first place.

One other negative evidence proposal is sometimes made, for so called *indirect negative evidence*. The idea is that children do not make certain kinds of mistakes because they never hear the ungrammatical forms produced by anyone else. In other words, children must notice the non-occurrence of certain sentence types and conclude that they are not allowed. This proposal runs into difficulties because of its vagueness. Since it is quite clear that children do in fact produce utterances which they have never heard and which are ungrammatical for adults, we would need a theory which would explain why children notice the non-occurrence of some sentence types but not others. Indeed, it appears that the child would have to have advance knowledge of what non-occurring sentences to look out for, which undermines the idea that indirect negative evidence can replace innate knowledge.[5] Furthermore, learners make many correct generalizations which go beyond the data they are exposed to, something that the indirect negative evidence proposal would preclude (i.e. non-occurrence of grammatical sentences would lead to them being treated as ungrammatical).

1.5 Evidence from child language

Our discussion of the various problems with input has focussed on three issues: underdetermination, degeneracy and the lack of negative evidence. Even though attempts have been made to argue that the latter two problems do not in fact exist and hence that there is no need for an innate component, these attempts underestimate the first problem, which is at the heart of arguments for UG.

In all three cases, we are making assumptions based on a comparison of adult knowledge and the presumed linguistic input to the first language learner. The mismatch between input received and knowledge attained motivates proposals for Universal Grammar. There is another, complementary, way of proceeding. That is, assuming (on the basis of such arguments) that there must be innate linguistic principles guiding language acquisition, one can look for evidence as to whether children are indeed guided by such principles. If so, we expect certain kinds of linguistic knowledge to be available to them without learning. For example, we expect children not to make errors which violate principles of UG, to know (unconsciously) that certain sentences are ungrammatical because they violate principles of UG, and to reject certain interpretations of sentences as impossible. A number of researchers have looked at L1 acquisition from this perspective, devising methodologies to test whether or not young children are constrained by principles of UG (e.g. Crain and Fodor, in press; papers in Lust 1986, 1987; Otsu 1981; papers in Roeper and Williams 1987; papers in Tavakolian 1981). Thus the logical arguments generate specific hypotheses about acquisition which in turn help to confirm the general claim that L1 acquisition is guided by innate principles.

1.6 Alternative views of universals and innateness

The solution offered by generative grammar to the acquisition problem is that the child does not come to the acquisition task equipped solely with an ability to extract generalizations from input data. Rather, specific linguistic principles are built in, in the form of UG. These severely constrain the types of analyses available to the child and dictate the kinds of hypotheses that will be made. UG provides a kind of blueprint as to what the grammar will be like, but details can only be filled in by input from the language being learned. From the outset the child is predisposed to deal with language input differently from other kinds of data and to deal with it in particular ways. The innate principles dictate the options open to the child; certain kinds of analyses (or grammars) will be ruled out out of hand (e.g. a grammar with rules which switch the first and last word). This explains why the errors that children make are far more limited in extent than might otherwise be expected.

Formal linguists are not the only researchers to have argued that language acquisition must be guided by innate principles of some kind. In developmental psycholinguistics, there have been numerous studies of similarities in the linguistic behaviour of different children, growing up in different communities and learning different languages. It is well known that different children show similar acquisition sequences and make the same kinds of errors, and that this is true cross-linguistically. This suggests that children must be driven by internal factors, since it is unlikely that all children have similar environmental experiences. Many argue that there must be a universal explanation for this behaviour, without accepting that this takes the form of UG, for example, Bates and MacWhinney (1987), Slobin (1986), who attribute the universality to functional and processing principles available to children. The focus of this book is on universal linguistic principles, rather than universal processing principles, although the two are not incompatible: it is likely that some aspects of acquisition are explained by UG, some by processing principles, some by neither of these.

There are also researchers who would like to be able to reduce principles of UG to other more general, non-linguistic cognitive principles (see Atkinson 1982 for discussion). There are two problems with such proposals, one theoretical, one practical. At the theoretical level, these attempts usually overlook the fact that the linguistic phenomena to be accounted for appear to be unique to language; there do not seem to be any equivalent principles in other cognitive domains, suggesting that specifically linguistic principles are required to explain them (but see O'Grady 1987 for a very interesting recent attempt to derive abstract linguistic knowledge from cognitive principles which are innate but not specifically linguistic.[6]) At the practical level, even if it should turn out that linguistic principles are ultimately reducible to something else, at the present time we have little idea what they might be reducible to; it is only by focussing on language as such that we have some idea of what is at stake, of the potential nature of the explanation.

1.7 Use of language

We have not yet considered Chomsky's third question, *How is knowledge of language put to use?* Chomsky makes a distinction between *competence* and *performance*, between theories of our underlying knowledge and theories which account for our use of that knowledge. A theory of linguistic competence will be one component in a theory of language use. Other theories will also be required, such as theories of language processing, pragmatics, and sociolinguistics. Theories of language use are excluded from theories of linguistic competence not because they are considered to be unimportant but because they embrace different phenomena requiring different types of explanation. (Indeed, they may involve different kinds of competence.)

There is a common misconception of the competence/performance distinction in the second language acquisition field. Chomskyan theory is often rejected because it does not consider explanations of learner behaviour (including variability in performance) to fall properly within the domain of knowledge of language (e.g. Ellis 1986, Tarone 1988). Within Chomskyan theory, learner behaviour is assumed to belong to a theory of use. It has been shown that there are a number of sociolinguistic variables which lead to use of some forms over others (cf. Labov 1972); a theory of use might be concerned with internal and external conditions that lead people to tap different aspects of their competence on different occasions. But the conditions that govern use are not themselves part of competence (for further discussion see Gregg 1988b, 1989; Sharwood Smith, to appear). Universal Grammar is concerned only with explaining aspects of linguistic competence and accounting for how it is acquired. When we look at the potential role of UG in second language acquisition, therefore, we shall not consider many aspects of second language performance, important though these are.

1.8 The content of Universal Grammar

As we have seen, arguments for Universal Grammar are motivated by a consideration of Chomsky's second question, *How is knowledge of language acquired?* Proposals for UG in turn affect the answer to his first question, *What constitutes knowledge of language?* since our knowledge of language includes both the innate universal principles that form the content of UG and language specific knowledge that is acquired with the aid of these principles.

What exactly is the content of UG? This is a question that is the focus of current linguistic theory, which tries to specify principles and parameters that underlie linguistic competence. Theories of UG have changed considerably in recent years. Much of the work that will be discussed in this book is done within the framework of Government-Binding (GB) theory (Chomsky 1981a). In this section, a brief overview of GB theory will be given.

Crucial concepts in GB theory are levels and subsystems, or modules. Modules contain principles which provide constraints on what goes on at the different levels. The constraints are assumed to hold in all languages (with certain qualifications which will be discussed later) and to embrace a

wide range of phenomena. Examples will be drawn from English and will
be very limited in scope. The intention here is simply to present some ter-
minology and some of the main concepts, especially those that have been
investigated in the second language acquisition context.

1.8.1 *Levels of representation*

The form of any grammar is dictated by UG. A grammar has a number of
different levels: D-structure, S-structure, phonetic form (PS) and logical
form (LF). These are usually represented as follows:

(27)

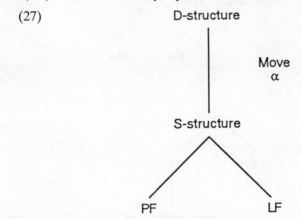

D-structure is the level at which certain relationships are represented,
particularly grammatical and thematic relationships. There is one movement rule (or transformation), *move α*, which moves syntactic categories
out of their D-structure positions, leaving an empty category (a trace)
behind to mark the original position of the moved element. S-structure is
the level that represents these effects of *move α*. For example, the embedded clause in (28a) would have a D-structure as in (28b) and an S-structure
as in (28c):[7]

(28) a.   I wonder what John found
      b.

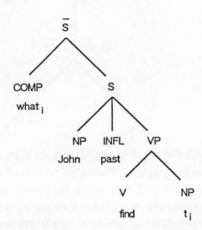

      c.

In (28), *what* is the object of the lower verb *find* and it is thematically dependent on it, having the thematic (θ) role of theme. This is represented at D-structure by having *what* as the NP constituent of the VP. At S-structure, *what* has moved into COMP but the coindexed trace remains, indicating the position that it originally occupied.

PF is a level at which various phonological and phonetic operations take place, together with certain stylistic rules, such as *wanna*-contraction discussed in 1.4.1.1; it will not be discussed further. LF is a level of representation for those aspects of meaning that relate to sentence structure, such as scope of quantifiers. The rule *move* α also mediates between S-structure and LF. For example, the LF representation of (29a) would be something like (29b):

(29) a.   Mary likes everyone
      b.   Everyone$_i$ Mary likes t$_i$

In addition to these levels is the lexicon, where lexical items (words, affixes, idioms) are stored, together with information about such properties as their syntactic categories, subcategorization requirements, thematic properties, morphological and phonological structure, and meanings. A number of morphological and phonological operations may in fact take place in the lexicon, although theories differ over this question.

1.8.2 *Subsystems of UG*

Move α is a general rule; it can move anything anywhere. It replaces the very detailed and specific rules of earlier versions of generative grammar. There is now assumed to be only one simple rule for the child to acquire, rather than a number of complex rules, thus reducing the learning problem. However, because of its simplicity and generality, *move* α overgenerates, producing structures which are not, in fact, permitted. For example, *move* α could generate a number of the ungrammatical sentences that were considered in 1.4. For this reason, UG is assumed to consist of a number of different principles, or constraints, which together have the effect of preventing various kinds of overgeneration. These constraints form different subsystems (or modules) of UG.

There is no one level at which all principles operate. Some operate at D-structure (e.g. X bar theory, theta theory), some at S-structure (e.g. Subjacency), some at LF (e.g. the Empty Category Principle). Some may operate at more than one level (e.g. the Binding Theory), or at all levels (e.g. the Projection Principle). Below we shall briefly discuss the major modules and constraints of current GB theory.

1.8.2.1 *X bar theory*
Phrase-structures are constrained by X bar theory which specifies the hierarchical structure holding between heads of phrases and their specifiers and complements. The basic idea is that different phrasal categories or maximal projections, such as noun phrase (N″), verb phrase (V″), preposi-

tional phase (P″) and adjective phrase (A″), all conform to a general schema. They must contain a head (X = N, V, P and A respectively); any complements (e.g. relative clauses in NPs, direct objects in VPs, objects of the preposition in PPs) will be sisters to the head. The head and complements together form the X bar (X′) level. Specifiers (such as determiners) will be outside this level. The overall schema can be seen in (30):

(30)

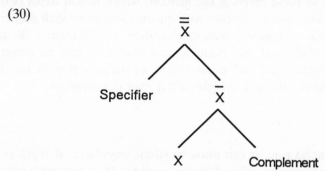

The lexical entries of various heads will include information about their argument structure, particularly the kinds of syntactic category that can serve as their complements (subcategorization information) and the thematic roles (theta or θ roles) that these complements can have. For example, the verb *find* subcategorizes for an NP as its complement, which has the θ role of *theme*. In addition, verbs assign a θ role to their subjects, which are outside of their maximal projection. These are sometimes called *external arguments*, in contrast to complements which are *internal arguments*.

1.8.2.2 *Theta Theory*

All NPs in a sentence need a theta (θ) role,[8] and all the θ roles of a verb must be assigned. These requirements are achieved by the Theta Criterion which says that each argument bears one and only one θ role, and each θ role is assigned to one and only one argument. (31a) is ungrammatical because *seems* does not have a θ role to assign to the subject position, leaving *John* without a θ role. (31b) is ungrammatical because *found* does have a θ role to assign to its complement but there is no NP to receive it.

    (31) a.   *John seems that he is sad
           b.   *John found

1.8.2.3 *The Projection Principle*

The Projection Principle is a constraint on the mappings between the different levels. It is a requirement that subcategorization and thematic information contained in the lexicon should be represented at each syntactic level, i.e. at D-structure, S-structure and LF. To return to our example of the verb *find*, this verb's lexical entry contains the information that it subcategorizes for an NP with the θ role of theme. The Projection Principle requires that the representations of any sentences containing this verb preserve this information in some form. Consider again sentence (28), repeated here as (32):

(32) I wonder what John found

The D-structure of (32) was given in (28b), where the tree shows the verb to take an NP object. The S-structure was given in (28c), where a trace marks the position from which the word *what* has moved. The Projection Principle crucially depends on empty categories like traces, since these allow the original lexical structure to be represented.

1.8.2.4 *Subjacency*

Subjacency is a principle which provides constraints on how far categories may be moved by *move α*, i.e. it places bounds on movement. In 1.4.1.3, we saw that certain kinds of movement are not in fact possible in English, that *move α* cannot take any *wh*-element and move it anywhere. Sentences like those in (33) are ungrammatical:

(33) a. *What did Mary wonder whether John bought?
     b. *What did Mary believe the claim that John saw?

Subjacency stipulates that any application of *move α* may not cross more than one *bounding node* at a time, where the bounding nodes for English are S and NP.[9] In (34), the relevant bounding nodes for (33) have been included. The trace marks the original site of the *wh*-word:

(34) a. *What$_i$ [$_S$ did Mary wonder [$_{S'}$ whether [$_S$ John bought t$_i$]]]
     b. *What$_i$ [$_S$ did Mary believe [$_{NP}$ the claim [$_{S'}$ that [$_S$ John saw t$_i$]]]]

In (34a), the *wh*-word has crossed two S nodes, in (34b) it has crossed two S nodes and an NP node, in both cases violating Subjacency.

There are occasions when *wh*-words can move quite a long distance; this is because they can move into the COMP position in one movement and then subsequently hop into another COMP position, provided COMP is not already occupied by some other *wh*-word. In (35), *what* can move into the COMP of the embedded clause (which does not already contain a *wh*-word), thereby crossing only one bounding node, namely S, and from there it can move into the higher COMP at the front of the sentence, again crossing only one bounding node. Subjacency is not violated with this kind of COMP-to-COMP movement.

(35)   What$_i$ [$_S$ did Mary think [$_{S'}$ t$_i$ that [$_S$ John bought t$_i$]]]

In (34a), on the other hand, the lower COMP is occupied by *whether* and so cannot also be temporarily occupied by *what*. In (34b), *what* could pass through the lower COMP but then still has to cross two bounding nodes, NP and S, in violation of Subjacency.

1.8.2.5 *Case Theory*

Case Theory provides a constraint on S-structures, by means of the Case Filter, a requirement that all lexical NPs have abstract Case (i.e. empty categories are excluded). Verbs and prepositions assign case to their objects, and INFL (if it is tensed) assigns case to subjects. The sentence in (36a) is ungrammatical because it violates the Case Filter; *John* cannot receive case from the adjective or the infinitival *to*, neither of which are case assigners. In (36b), on the other hand, *John* has moved into the subject position of the main clause, where it gets case from INFL.

(36)   a.   *It is likely John to be there
      b.   John is likely *t* to be there

In many languages there is an Adjacency Condition on Case Assignment (Stowell 1981; Chomsky 1981a, 1986), which is a requirement that an NP receiving case must be next to its case assigner. This explains why (37a) is unacceptable, in contrast to (37b):

(37)   a.   *Mary likes very much apples
      b.   Mary likes apples very much

1.8.2.6 *C-command and Government*

C-command and Government are two very important concepts in GB theory which are crucial in a number of the subsystems. For example, there is normally a requirement of government on θ-role assignment and case assignment; the θ or case assigner governs the assignee.

C-command is defined as follows: a category α c-commands another category β if and only if the first branching node dominating α also dominates β.[10] To see how this works, consider the tree in (38):

(38)

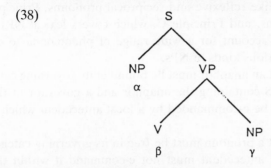

The first branching node dominating the NP α is the S. This S also dominates the V β and the NP γ. Therefore, α c-commands both β and γ. β and γ, on the other hand, do not c-command α, since the first branching node dominating them is VP, which does not dominate α. They do, however, c-command each other.

For α to govern β, α must c-command β, α and β must be in the same maximal projection, and no maximal projection may intervene between β and α. In (39), the verb α governs the NP β because the relevant criteria are met: the verb c-commands the NP following it, and the first maximal projection (VP) dominating the NP also dominates the V. On the other hand, α does not govern the NP γ because α does not c-command γ and a maximal projection, the VP, intervenes between them. α also does not govern the NP δ, even though α c-commands δ and they are both within the VP, because the PP, a maximal projection, intervenes between them.

(39)

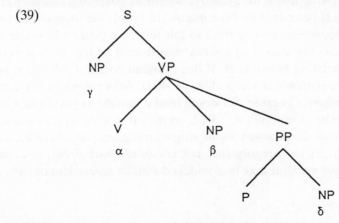

1.8.2.7 *Binding Theory*

The Binding Theory constrains the relationships between various kinds of nounphrases. The theory consists of three principles, Principle A, which is concerned with anaphors like reflexive and reciprocal pronouns, Principle B, which handles pronouns, and Principle C, which covers lexical NPs.[11] Together these principles account for a wide range of phenomena to do with the distribution of various kinds of NPs.

Principle A states that an anaphor must be bound in its governing category (the smallest NP or S containing the anaphor and a governor of the anaphor). That is, it must be c-commanded by a local antecedent which is coindexed with it.

Principle B states that a pronoun must be free in its governing category. That is, its coindexed antecedent must not c-command it within the same clause or NP.

Principle C states that lexical NPs must be free i.e. they must not be c-commanded by a coindexed antecedent at all, no matter how far away.

Consider the sentences in (40). We are concerned with the reasons why the coindexed NPs in each sentence can or cannot be coreferential. In each sentence, the governing category has been bracketed.

(40)   a.   [John$_i$ saw himself$_i$]
           b.   *[He$_i$ saw John$_i$]
           c.   *[John$_i$ saw him$_i$]
           d.   *John$_i$ said [that Fred hurt himself$_i$]
           e.   John said [that Fred$_i$ hurt himself$_i$]
           f.   John$_i$ said [that Fred hurt him$_i$]
           g. *He$_i$ said [that Fred hurt John$_i$]

In (40a), *John* c-commands the reflexive within its governing category and so the sentence is permitted by Principle A. In (40b), the pronoun c-commands the name, which must be free, so this sentence violates Principle C. In (40c), *John* c-commands the pronoun, which must be free in its governing category, violating Principle B. If this pronoun does not refer to *John*, it is free and the sentence is acceptable. In (40d), *John* cannot be the antecedent of the reflexive because this would bind it outside its governing category, which violates Condition A. (40e), on the other hand, is grammatical because *Fred* binds the pronoun within its governing category. In (40f), *him* is free in its governing category (i.e. not coindexed with *Fred*), in accordance with Condition B. It may be coindexed with an antecedent outside of its governing category, such as *John*. In (40g), *he* c-commands *John*, in violation of Condition C. In all the sentences except (40b) and (40g), both *John* and *Fred* are free, as required by Condition C.

1.8.2.8 *Empty categories and the Empty Category Principle*

There are four different kinds of empty category in GB theory. Two of them are traces left behind after movement, namely *wh*-traces and NP-traces. We have already seen a number of examples of *wh*-traces, which mark the origin of a moved *wh*-word, for example in (28c). Similarly, NP traces mark the site of moved NPs, as in (36b). These two kinds of traces have rather different properties, which will not be dealt with here. They are both subject to the Empty Category Principle (ECP), which states that a trace must be properly governed. Proper government is similar to government: α properly governs β if and only if α governs β and α is a lexical category (N, V, A, P) or α and β are coindexed.

Certain oddities in the distribution of English complementizers were discussed in 1.4.1.2 In particular, a subject-object asymmetry was noted with respect to the presence of the complementizer *that*. When the subject of an embedded question is extracted, *that* must be deleted, whereas when an object is extracted, it is optional, as was seen in (18) and (19), repeated here in (41):

(41) a.   Who$_i$ do you think that Mary met t$_i$ yesterday?
      b.   Who$_i$ do you think Mary met t$_i$ yesterday?
      c.   Who$_i$ do you think t$_i$ arrived yesterday?
      d.   *Who$_i$ do you think that t$_i$ arrived yesterday?

In other words, the complementizer *that* cannot be followed by a trace; this is sometimes called the *that-trace effect*. The ungrammaticality of (41d) is due to a violation of the ECP. In (41a) and (41b) the trace is properly governed by the verb *met*, which is a lexical category governing it, so the ECP is satisfied. To understand what happens in (41c) and (41d), it is important to remember that *wh*-words have to pass through COMP, in order not to violate Subjacency; another trace is left in COMP. This trace is coindexed with the original trace. In (41c), this trace properly governs the original one because it is coindexed with it and c-commands it, and they are within the same maximal projection, namely S', as shown in (42a). However, in (41d), proper government is not possible because the intermediate trace in COMP does not c-command the original trace, as can be seen in (42b):

(42)   a.

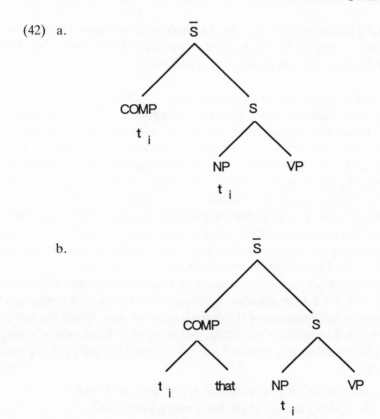

b.

In (42b), COMP is the first branching node dominating the intermediate trace and this node does not also dominate the trace in subject position in the embedded clause. Thus, sentences like (41d) violate the ECP.

Besides traces, there are two other kinds of empty category, which are not subject to the ECP. These are PRO and *pro*. *Pro* is an empty pronominal and does not occur in English. It is found as the subject of the sentence in 'prodrop' languages, e.g. Italian or Spanish, and also in other positions, including the object position, in languages like Japanese and Chinese. PRO occurs only in ungoverned positions, such as the subject of infinitives and gerunds, as in (43):

(43)   a.   John decided PRO to leave
      b.   After PRO eating, Mary left the house

1.9 Principles and parameters

Government-Binding Theory is one formulation of a principles and parameters approach to UG. It is important to realize that although the principles of UG are universal, this does not mean that every principle necessarily operates in every language. This is perhaps easier to understand by means of an example from phonetics, where there is assumed to be a universal set of phonetic features (listed in UG). Individual languages have a phonetic inventory which makes use of a subset of the full set of features; as a result, different languages make use of different sounds. The features of any one language do not constitute the full set but are drawn from it. Similarly, there will be cases in syntax where languages do not make use of all the available principles of UG. One way in which languages differ, then, is in terms of which of the set of possible universals they actually realize. For instance, Subjacency will not operate in languages without syntactic movement rules, since Subjacency is a constraint on movement and is of no relevance in the absence of movement. We would not, however, expect to find languages with syntactic movement but without Subjacency. Although languages vary in terms of their syntactic properties, principles are fixed and must apply to all languages which exhibit the relevant properties.

Another kind of variation between languages is also found, which is captured by the concept of parameterization. Certain principles of UG differ in the way they work from language to language. One does not want to have to say that these differences have to be learned, since they involve very subtle and complex properties which are thought to be unlearnable, for the reasons discussed above. The differences are accounted for by incorporating a limited number of options into UG. Parameterized principles which exhibit such options are called *parameters* and the different values of the options are called *parameter settings*. Parameters account for clusters of properties, which superficially might seem to be unrelated. Parameters give the child advance knowledge of what the possibilities will be, that is, they limit the range of hypotheses that have to be considered. The function of the input data in language acquisition is to help to fix one of the possible settings. This is called *triggering*. In other words, the input helps to make the choice between the various built-in settings.

One example of a parameter concerns the ordering relationship of heads and their complements. On the whole, languages fall into two types: head-initial, where the ordering is head-complement, and head-final, where the ordering is complement-head. The point of interest is that this applies across categories. In a head-initial language, the complements of the verb (such as the direct object and subcategorized prepositional phrases) will occur after the verb, the complements of the noun (such as relative or appositive clauses) after the noun, the complements of prepositions and adjectives after the preposition or adjective; in head final languages, complements will all precede their heads.

Head-position is a parameter with two values; its settings are head-initial or head-final (Chomsky 1986; Travis 1984). This parameter accounts for the ordering of heads and complements across many different phrasal categories.[12] Suppose that a child is learning a head-initial language like English, then there are many simple sentences that can trigger the appropriate value for the parameter. A sentence with verb object word order shows that verbs precede their complements, and can be used to set the parameter to head-initial, for example. Once the parameter has been set on the basis of evidence relating to one phrasal category, it does not have to be reset for the other phrasal categories; the rest follow as an automatic consequence of the head-initial setting of the parameter, and do not have to be triggered or learned individually.

1.10 What UG does not do

So far, we have seen that UG consists of principles and parameters which help to account for the child's acquisition of complex and subtle linguistic phenomena which go beyond the primary input. It is not, however, intended that UG should account for all aspects of L1 acquisition. Properties that are specific to a language will have to be learned. These include much of the lexicon: words and their meanings will have to be learned, together with their syntactic categories and subcategorization requirements.

Nor is it the case that every phenomenon in language acquisition that seems to be universal must be explained in terms of UG. For a number of years, L1 acquisition research, and also L2, concentrated on the order of acquisition of certain inflectional morphemes (e.g. Brown 1973; Dulay and Burt 1974a). An order common to many different children was found. Although this clearly requires explanation, it is not necessarily a UG-based one. UG does not have anything to say about morpheme acquisition as such: morphemes are lexical items; they are language specific and have to be learned. It is also not clear to what extent UG can explain acquisition orders in general. Some acquisition order phenomena do appear to be consequences of UG (as we shall see when we look at the issue of markedness), but by no means all of them are. UG provides constraints on acquisition stages (they must observe principles of UG) without necessarily explaining why stages occur in the order that they do.

1.11 Conclusion

We have seen that arguments for UG derive their force by looking at the final, adult grammar, in all its complexity. They stem from the claim that the input to the language learner underdetermines the end result, that the input is insufficiently precise to account for linguistic competence. Generative grammar focusses on the properties of a formal system, or grammar, and the question of how this system can be acquired; it puts to one side other aspects of language and the role of factors that are not crucial to these formal properties. This does not mean that such factors (e.g. discourse and pragmatics) should not form part of an overall theory of language, nor does it mean that an overall theory of language acquisition should ignore them. However, the current trend both in linguistics and in cognitive psychology is to assume that global theories that try to account for everything should in fact be broken down into sub-theories, each with its own domain. The theory of Universal Grammar is one such sub-theory, accounting for a limited but crucial domain. In line with this thinking, we shall focus on only one potential component of a theory of second language acquisition and will omit many issues, not because they are not important but because they do not happen to fall within the scope of Universal Grammar.

1.12 Further reading

For readers who are interested in pursuing some or all of the issues raised in this chapter, the following are recommended:
i.   *Smith and Wilson* (1979) and *Newmeyer* (1983) present and justify the Chomskyan approach to language very clearly, in fairly general terms. They do not assume technical knowledge of generative grammar.

ii.   Government Binding theory is presented in technical detail in *Radford* (1981, 1988), *Van Riemsdijk and Williams* (1986) and in *Lasnik and Uriagereka* (1988). *Sells* (1985) and *Cook* (1988) provide excellent overviews of GB theory, which will probably be of sufficient detail for the reader of this book. Chomsky himself is very hard to read, especially for those without a background in linguistics. Periodically, he writes books aimed at a more general audience, for example *Chomsky* (1975, 1980, 1986).

iii.   Questions pertaining to linguistic theory and L1 acquisition, especially the logical problem of acquisition, written with the non-specialist in mind, are addressed in *Lightfoot* (1982), *Goodluck* (1986 and in press), and *White* (1982). Theoretical and empirial papers on L1 acquisition within this framework are to be found in *Lust* (1986, 1987), *Roeper and Williams* (1987) and *Tavakolian* (1981).

Notes to Chapter 1

1.   A * indicates that a form is ungrammatical or impossible.

2.   This model makes it look as if internalizing a grammar is instantaneous, which is clearly not the case.

3.   It also applies to *have to*, *used to*, etc.

4.   We are concerned with the interpretation of the sentences which involves reading the letter, rather than reading in general.

5.   Chomsky (1981a) suggests that this could be part of UG, specifically parameter theory. If learners have a very limited number of options built in, they can check for the non-occurrence of sentence types relating to one of the options.

6.   What makes O'Grady's book particularly interesting is the fact that he is well aware of the problem of underdetermination and tries to show how his cognitive principles can derive all the abstract linguistic phenomena that linguists are interested in. This is a welcome change from other proposals for cognitive principles underlying acquisition which tend to be vague.

7.   I assume familiarity with categories such as S, NP and VP. COMP=complementizer and INFL=inflection, two categories which are of considerable importance in GB theory.

8.   With the exception of pleonastic pronouns like *it* and *there*.

9.   According to some analyses, S' is a bounding node as well (Chomsky 1981b; Sportiche 1981).

10.   There are a number of definitions of C-command and Government in the syntactic literature, which share the same basic ideas although differing as to details.

11.   Empty categories also fall under the binding principles, but I will not go into details here.

12.   There are languages which, on the surface at least, do not show consistent head-comple-
       ment orders. It must be borne in mind that the Head-position Parameter affects D-struc-
       ture orders, not S-structure, and that certain derived orders show up at S-structure which
       are not the same as the underlying order.

2 The logical problem of second language acquisition

2.1 Introduction

In the previous chapter, a number of arguments were presented for an innate language faculty, Universal Grammar, which constrains L1 acquisition, and which provides a partial answer to Chomsky's second question *How is knowledge of language acquired?*[1] In this chapter, we shall consider whether a parallel case can be made for L2 acquisition, whether the proposal that language acquirers are equipped with innate structure in the form of UG still holds true of non-primary acquisition.

2.2 L2 knowledge of language

2.2.1 *Interlanguage grammars*

Asking whether UG plays a part in second language acquisition presupposes that Chomsky's first question, *What constitutes knowledge of language?*, will receive a similar answer in both L1 and L2 acquisition. It only makes sense to ask if knowledge of language is acquired in a similar fashion if that knowledge has common properties in both contexts. As we have seen, knowledge of language for the native speaker is represented in the form of a mental grammar, an abstract system of principles and rules. In effect, then, we are assuming that competence in a second language will also be represented in the form of an internalized grammar. This does not, however, mean that the form and content of the internalized grammar must be totally identical in the two situations.

So far, the fact that L1 and L2 learners go through acquisition stages has been ignored. Learners do not acquire competence instantaneously. This means that the question *What constitutes knowledge of language?* must be reconsidered in the context of language acquirers. Competence changes over time; nevertheless, at any particular point in the acquisition process, the learner can be said to have an internalized grammar, which constitutes his or her current competence, the current attempt to organize the input data.

The idea that the L2 learner's competence can be represented by a series of internalized grammars is not new. It underlies the interlanguage (IL) hypothesis, the assumption being that the learner's approach to the L2 is systematic and rule-governed, and that this is best accounted for by a series of transitional systems, or interlanguage grammars (Adjémian 1976; Corder 1967; Selinker 1972). Although an interlanguage grammar (ILG) differs in a number of respects from the grammar of a native speaker, it nevertheless represents knowledge of the language, in that it accounts for the learner's interim competence by means of an abstract rule system.

2.2.2 *L2 knowledge and L2 use of language*

Another assumption that will be made throughout this book is that there is a crucial distinction between competence and performance in L2 acquisition. Language use by an L2 learner will not only reflect the currently internalized competence, the ILG, but will also reflect performance variables which are not part of that competence, although they may interact with it. For example, the informal rule of *wanna*-contraction was discussed in Chapter 1. This rule is part of the competence of some native speakers of English. The competence of these speakers includes the contraction rule (appropriately constrained via UG). This is not, however, a rule that they use all the time: it is much more likely to be used in informal circumstances than in formal ones. The fact that this rule is used under varying conditions does not affect the native speaker's knowledge of language. The rule itself is part of competence; the conditions governing its use are not.

Similar situations will arise in L2 acquisition, where learners happen, on particular occasions, not to make use of knowledge which is in fact part of their interlanguage competence. Indeed, as we shall see, devising appropriate methods to tap the L2 learner's competence, while abstracting away from performance phenomena, is not an easy task, but it is crucial to be able to do this in order to investigate the role of UG in second language acquisition.[2]

2.3 The logical problem of L2 acquisition

Assuming the above parallels between L1 and L2 knowledge and use of language, another similarity between L1 and L2 acquisition can be considered. The L2 learner's task bears a strong resemblance to that of the L1 learner. L2 learners are also faced with the problem of making sense of input data, of coming up with a system which will account for that data, and which will allow them to understand and produce structures of the L2. Thus, their task can be conceived of as follows, equivalent to the L1 acquisition task:

(1)

L2 Input ⟶ L2 Grammar

For the moment, possible differences in the end results of L1 and L2 acquisition will be ignored, particularly the fact that many L2 learners do not attain a grammar which is effectively identical to native speakers.

UG was motivated for L1 acquisition by a consideration of the projection problem. As discussed in Chapter 1, there is a mismatch between the kind of input available to L1 acquirers and their ultimate attainment; despite the fact that certain properties of language are not explicit in the input, native speakers end up with a complex grammar that goes far beyond the input, resulting in knowledge of grammaticality, ungrammaticality, ambiguity, paraphrase relations, and various subtle and complex phenomena, suggesting that universal principles must mediate acquisition and shape knowledge of language.

The same issue will now be considered for L2 acquisition, namely whether there is a mismatch between the input that L2 learners receive and their ultimate attainment. If the three problems with input still hold in this context, then it is possible that UG also plays a role, that innate linguistic principles mediate L2 acquisition, helping to solve the L2 projection problem, as in (2):

(2)

L2 Input ⟶ UG ⟶ L2 Grammar

Although a demonstration of an L2 projection problem motivates claims for UG, two alternatives suggest themselves. One is that the L2 projection problem might solved without UG, for example, with the use of knowledge drawn from the L1 grammar. The other is that the projection problem might not be solved at all; L2 learners may never attain a grammar which goes beyond the input in any significant respect. These alternatives will be discussed in 2.5.

2.3.1 *Underdetermination*

In order to decide whether there is indeed an L2 projection problem, we must consider whether the L2 input underdetermines the grammar achieved by the L2 learner. For the sake of the argument, reasonably successful L2 acquirers[3] will be considered, who have had naturalistic L2 acquisition, outside the language classroom, in order to put to one side the fact that L2 learners may get input in a rather different form from L1 learners, which will be dealt with below.

It seems most unlikely that L2 input will contain explicit information about the kinds of properties of language discussed in Chapter 1.4.1. Information about when contraction is and is not possible, when the complementizer must be obligatorily absent, and about the binding requirements on pronouns, as well as many other subtle phenomena, is, as we have seen, not available in the primary input to L1 acquirers. There is no reason to assume any difference in naturalistic primary input to L2 acquirers. If there is no essential difference between L1 and L2 input, then L2 input will underdetermine the L2 grammar in precisely the same way that L1 input underdetermines the L1 grammar. In that case, we potentially have the same projection problem as in L1 acquisition, namely that knowledge is attained which goes beyond the input and which could not be acquired on the basis of general learning strategies or problem-solving.

This, of course, presupposes that the end result of the L2 acquisition process is indeed a complex grammar which shows the relevant properties. In other words, it assumes that the underlying competence attained by second language learners shows evidence of the same (or similar) subtlety and complexity as that of native speakers, that L2 learners observe principles like Subjacency, the Empty Category Principle, and the Binding Theory, as well as any other principles of UG.

One recent paper (Coppieters 1986) looks in some detail at the internalized knowledge of adults who have been assessed as having near native-speaker competence in their second language (acquired as adults) and who can be assumed to have completed the L2 acquisition process. Looking at their competence is comparable to looking at the competence of adult native speakers, which is how linguists arrive at the putative properties of UG. Coppieters found interesting differences between these subjects and monolingual controls, especially as regards semantic factors relating to choice of certain tenses, pronouns and adjective positions, i.e., properties of language that would not necessarily stem from UG. However, for the few principles of UG which were included in his investigation, the subjects and controls performed very similarly. That is, these L2 learners appeared to have internalized complex and subtle knowledge not obviously available in the input.

Of course, many L2 learners never attain a point where they are judged as being close to native speakers. Nevertheless, even if the L2 learner's grammar is not native-like, it can often be highly sophisticated and complex, revealing linguistic properties which could not have been induced directly from the input data. If the L2 learner goes beyond input, even though not as far as the native speaker, then there is potentially an L2 equivalent of the projection problem. That is, knowledge is attained on the basis of impoverished input, and this requires an explanation.

2.3.2 *Degeneracy*

Another deficiency of the input that originally led to arguments for UG was the alleged degeneracy of some of the input to L1 learners. If the input contains a mixture of grammatical and ungrammatical sentences, it makes it very much harder (if not impossible) to work out the underlying principles, because the ungrammatical sentences will obscure any generalizations that might otherwise be made on the basis of the grammatical sentences. As discussed in Chapter 1, a number of researchers have suggested that the input to young children is not in fact degenerate and that this lessens the need for an innate component (Brown 1977; McLaughlin 1987). Similarly, L2 learners often get non-degenerate input, in the form of *teacher-talk* or *foreigner-talk*. It has been argued that the existence of such input weakens the arguments for an innate component in L2 acquisition (e.g. Ellis 1986).

However, the existence of non-degenerate input does not solve the acquisition problem at all, as we have already seen. Grammatical input underdetermines our linguistic competence. This is just as true of L2 acquisition as it is of L1. Even if input consists only of short phrases and sentences which are totally grammatical, these will not allow a learner to induce the abstract properties of the internalized grammar, suggesting that knowledge of these abstract properties must be built in in some form. Simplified input is also only of limited value, since it does not contain information relevant to complex sentences, effectively depriving the learner of important information about language. Providing simplified input only puts off the issue of acquiring complex structure; it does not solve it.

2.3.3 *Negative evidence*

The third deficiency of input in L1 acquisition is the lack of negative evidence. A lack of reliable negative evidence motivated the argument that children must be endowed with principles which give them advance knowledge of ungrammaticality, and which prevent many incorrect hypotheses from ever being entertained; hence knowledge of ungrammaticality is not acquired by means of negative evidence, and incorrect hypotheses do not have to be eliminated by means of correction.

L1 and L2 acquisition are, superficially at least, quite different in this respect. Many L2 learners do get negative evidence in the classroom. Correction is one source of negative evidence; so is explicit grammar teaching, since this often includes information about what structures are unacceptable in the language being learned. If L2 learners make use of this kind of evidence, it might be argued that they could home in on a reasonable approximation to the L2 grammar without one's having to assume much innate structure to guide them (e.g. Ellis 1986[4]). In other words, they could start off with overgeneral or incorrect rules, produce incorrect structures on the basis of these rules and revise their grammars on the basis of correction and explicit grammar teaching.

Once again, the availability of negative data does not allow the conclusion that innate constraints are not required. For negative evidence to be effective, it must be reliably available and it must be used. Not all L2 learners get negative evidence, and they cannot control when they get it. Those who get it do not necessarily take note of it. The fact that L1 and L2 acquisition differ with respect to the availability of this form of input does not mean that they necessarily differ with respect to internal mechanisms that govern language acquisition.

In any case, the crucial question for L2 acquisition (as it was for L1) is not the availability or non-availability of negative evidence but whether learners make certain errors in the first place. One can hardly be corrected for errors that one does not make. The competence of native speakers includes the unconscious knowledge that certain sentences are ungrammatical, i.e., sentences violating principles of UG. This knowledge is attained by children in an error-free fashion. L1 acquirers do not produce sentences violating principles of UG and then get corrected; rather, they never produce the violations in the first place. Although L2 learners make mistakes and are corrected in certain contexts, these mistakes do not appear to involve violations of principles of UG. Thus, the kind of negative evidence that L2 learners get is simply irrelevant to the issue of the L2 projection problem. It is not evidence that could give L2 learners the kind of abstract knowledge represented by principles of UG.

2.4 Some differences between L1 and L2 acquisition

In spite of similarities between L1 and L2 acquisition in terms of the acquisition task and the acquisition problem, there are of course considerable differences, which have been taken as evidence that L1 and L2 acquisition are fundamentally different as far as UG is concerned (Bley-Vroman 1989; Schachter 1988b). In this section, some differences between L1 and L2 acquisition will be reviewed. Although these differences are real, it will be suggested that they do not necessarily force us to abandon a role for UG in L2 acquisition.

2.4.1 *Degree of success*

An obvious difference between L1 and L2 acquisition is the degree of success attained by learners. All first language learners are totally successful, in that they acquire a grammar which makes their language virtually indistinguishable from that of other people who have grown up in the same speech community. In L2 acquisition, on the other hand, it is common for the learner to fail to acquire the target language fully; there are often clear differences between the output of the L2 learner and that of native speakers, and learners differ as to how successful they are.

Although it is the case that many L2 learners do not achieve complete success, this failure should not necessarily be attributed to the non-operation of UG. One of the most obvious differences between success in L1 and L2 acquisition is found in phonology; many L2 learners are unable to acquire an accurate L2 accent. Another problem area for L2 learners is the acquisition of inflectional morphology, where native-like language is notoriously hard to achieve. These differences, however, are irrelevant for the question of whether or not UG operates in L2 acquisition. Failure to achieve native-speaker-like pronunciation can be attributed at least in part to articulatory difficulties experienced by older learners; it tells us nothing about whether abstract principles and constraints of UG play a part in the learner's internalization of a grammar. Many properties of language are specific to individual languages and will have to be learned as such. This will include various lexical properties, both vocabulary and morphology. Failure or difficulty in acquiring these does not reflect adversely on the hypothesis that UG operates in L2 acquisition, because these are not aspects of language that stem from UG. In other words, the failure of L2 learners in certain aspects of phonology and morphology, in contrast to the success of L1 learners in these domains, certainly requires explanation, but not necessarily an explanation that depends on the presence or absence of UG.

Schachter (1988b) points out that L2 learners often fail to use structures derived by movement, such as clefts, topicalization, or raising. She suggests that this is another indication of lack of total success, which casts doubt on a central role for UG in L2 acquisition. However, it is quite clear that the competence of many L2 learners does include movement rules, since they produce structures like *wh*-questions, relative clauses, and passives, all of which are derived via the rule, *move α*. The difference, then, is that certain structures derived by movement are used less by L2 learners than by native speakers. These are performance differences and it is not at all clear that they stem from competence differences. In all of Schachter's examples, movement is optional. The observation that L2 learners fail to produce certain structures cannot be used to argue that L2 competence is fundamentally different from L1; one needs to know whether these learners also fail to comprehend the structures in question, and whether they are incapable of producing them (as opposed to choosing not to use them). One must be careful about conclusions drawn on the basis of spontaneous production data alone; these only give an incomplete window on competence.[5]

Indeed, the claim that L2 learners are not fully successful has to be reassessed in light of the hypothesis that UG may be involved in L2 acquisition. This is an issue that has to be investigated for the properties of language that UG is assumed to cover; not enough is yet known about whether the L2 learner's grammar includes the kind of complex knowledge that a native speaker has. If it does, then L2 learners achieve success in the relevant respects, even though they may not achieve success in other domains.

2.4.2 *Mother tongue*

Another obvious difference between L1 and L2 learners is that L2 learners know another language. Furthermore, it is often suggested that L2 learners whose L1 is related to their L2 have an advantage over learners whose L1 is unrelated (e.g. Corder 1978). However, prior knowledge of another language, or the existence of beneficial effects attributable to that language, does not constitute evidence that UG does not operate in L2 acquisition. What is required is a theory as to how UG interacts with existing knowledge, including the L1 grammar. The concept of parameterized principles provides a foundation for such a theory, as we shall see in later chapters.

2.4.3 *Fossilization*

Related to the issue of success is the question of fossilization (Selinker 1972). L2 learners often get 'stuck' at a point short of a native-like grammar and continue to produce non-target forms which are ineradicable. In many cases, fossilization involves the use of forms attributable to the mother tongue of the learner. Although L1 learners also pass through stages on the way to acquiring the final grammar, they do not get stuck at any of these interim stages.

Does the existence of fossilization force the conclusion that UG is ineffective? Again, the answer will depend on a theory of how UG works in L2 acquisition. In later chapters, it will be suggested that fossilization can be explained by considering how UG interacts with L1 knowledge and with input data from the L2. The fact that L2 learners already know another language prevents UG from operating as it would in L1 acquisition, but this is not the same as saying that it does not operate at all.

2.4.4 *Input*

L1 acquisition always takes place with naturalistic input, in contrast to L2 acquisition, where the input can vary considerably depending on the learning environment and teaching method. If acquisition depends on an interaction between UG and input, it is possible that lack of naturalistic input might make it harder for universal principles to be triggered, without forcing one to conclude that they are not available at all.

We have already mentioned the fact that L2 learners get more negative evidence than L1 learners, and that this is irrelevant as far as UG is concerned, unless L2 learners actually make errors that show that they are violating principles of UG. However, it will be suggested in Chapter 6, that there may be a role for negative evidence in L2 acquisition, to help eradicate errors which do not consist of violations of principles of UG but which involve incorrect parametric choices for the L2.

2.4.5 *Age*

The final difference between L1 and L2 acquisition that we shall touch on here concerns age. Most L2 learners are older than L1 learners, in many cases considerably so, and are more mature in terms of cognitive development. The effect of age in L2 acquisition is still a controversial topic. Some argue that older learners have an advantage (McLaughlin 1987), others that they have a disadvantage (Long 1988).

A number of researchers working on UG in L2 acquisition assume a role for UG in child L2 acquisition, but do not accept that it is involved in adult learning. Underlying this position is the assumption (a) that there is a critical period for language acquisition (Johnson and Newport 1989; Long 1988), and (b) that at the end of the critical period UG has somehow decayed or become inaccessible. It is, in fact, perfectly possible that (a) is true without (b) being so. In other words, there may indeed be a critical period without the end of it resulting in the loss of UG. This still remains a question for research, and much of the research to be discussed in this book focuses precisely on the question of whether UG is available to adult learners.

The argument that UG is unavailable to adults crucially depends on the assumption that UG is only a *language acquisition device*, helping the child to acquire language but playing no further role in adult knowledge of language. While this was a position consistent with earlier theories of UG, it is no longer so easily tenable. Given the way that UG is currently conceived, it appears that it is required to mediate adult knowledge of the mother tongue. UG serves as a language acquisition device in the sense that it severely restricts the kinds of grammar that the child hypothesizes in the course of acquisition, explaining why certain hypotheses are never entertained and why complex properties are acquired without any obvious evidence. But the role of UG does not finish when the course of language acquisition is over; since UG consists of negative constraints that, among other things, prevent ungrammatical sentences and allow some interpretations of sentences over others, these constraints must presumably be part of our adult competence as well. This means that differences between younger and older learners cannot be attributed to inaccessibility of UG.

It appears, then, that the various differences between L1 and L2 acquisition do not force us to abandon the possibility that UG mediates L2 acquisition. On the other hand, these differences suggest that the case in favour of UG is not clear cut either, and that theories that assume a role for UG must take these differences into consideration.

2.5 The L2 projection problem: alternative solutions

It was suggested above that the three problems with the input which were identified for L1 acquisition remain problematic for L2, that the two types of acquisition are similar in this respect. The most important of these problems is underdetermination. When one considers the L2 acquisition task and the assumed complexity of the grammar attained by successful L2 learners, this grammar appears to go far beyond the input, suggesting that there must be something like UG guiding L2 acquisition.

On the other hand, various differences between L1 and L2 acquisition have also been discussed. Two positions have emerged in response to these differences, both of which deny a significant role for UG. One is to acknowledge that L2 learners do attain appropriate knowledge of at least some abstract principles like the ECP or Subjacency, and to claim that this knowledge is attained via the mother tongue rather than directly via UG. The other is to admit that the L2 input shares the deficiencies of the L1 input but to deny the end result, i.e., to claim that L2 learners do not internalize a complex grammar which goes beyond input in the relevant respects. UG is assumed to be unavailable, and L2 acquisition takes place by means of very different learning procedures, such as problem-solving. Indeed, these two positions are not mutually exclusive and are often found together: some abstract principles are accessed via the L1, but where this is not possible, problem-solving procedures are used (e.g. Bley-Vroman 1989).

2.5.1 *The mother tongue grammar as a solution to the projection problem*

The first of these views sees the mother tongue of the learner as providing a partial solution to the L2 projection problem. If L2 learners do internalize grammars which go beyond the L2 input in the relevant respects, it might be that their L1 knowledge, rather than UG, allows them to do this, as shown in (3):

(3)

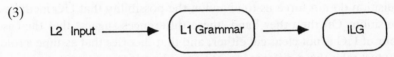

L2 Input ⟶ L1 Grammar ⟶ ILG

If UG operated in identical fashion from language to language, there would be no way of excluding this possibility. The ability to apply an abstract principle to the L2 might stem either directly from UG or from the L1.

In order to show that the L1 grammar cannot provide a solution to the L2 projection problem, it is necessary to eliminate the effects of the L1 in some way, to show that L2 input underdetermines ultimate attainment even if one takes mother tongue knowledge into consideration. If learners attain knowledge which could not have come via their mother tongue, and which could not have been induced from the input alone, arguments for a role for UG in L2 acquisition are strengthened. In 2.7.3, we will briefly consider cases which allow one to distinguish between L1-based knowledge and UG-based knowledge and which offer a principled way of ruling out the L1 as the only source of any complex knowledge that the L2 learner might attain.

2.5.2 *L2 acquisition as problem-solving*

Differences between L1 and L2 acquisition have also led to proposals that L2 acquisition is the result of problem-solving and hypothesis-testing, similar to learning in domains other than language (Bley-Vroman 1989). A hypothesis-testing account of language learning assumes that learners proceed on a basis of trial and error. They are exposed to input and come up with a hypothesis to account for this input. This hypothesis is used until evidence is encountered that suggests that the hypothesis is wrong. Another hypothesis for the data in question is then tried out, and so on until the learner hits on the right result.

Hypothesis-testing models have been rejected for L1 acquisition for a number of reasons. However, these same reasons make them, superficially at least, attractive as models of L2 learning. Firstly, hypothesis-testing cannot guarantee that learners will eventually hit on the right result; this appears to be a matter of chance: finding out that some hypothesis is wrong does not indicate which of many logically possible alternatives is the correct one. This is problematic for explaining L1 acquisition, where all learners do end up with the 'right' result, but could be used to explain the lack of success of many L2 learners. Secondly, hypothesis-testing crucially requires feedback, in the form of negative evidence; L1 learners do not appear to get such evidence to any significant extent, in contrast to L2 learners. Thirdly, hypothesis-testing models predict that learners should show radically different patterns of acquisition from each other, and different acquisition sequences, since each individual's hypotheses will be influenced by whether or not feedback was given at some particular point in the acquisition process, and by the order in which different utterances in the language were heard. L1 learners, however, show remarkably similar patterns and orders of acquisition. L2 learners show greater variation (although research that suggests that L2 learners go through similar acquisition sequences is potentially problematic for a hypothesis-testing view).

In spite of these superficially attractive features of hypothesis-testing as an account of L2 acquisition, one must not forget that the most crucial issue will, once again, be underdetermination. It is impossible that the kind of complex and subtle knowledge attained by native speakers could be arrived at by this means, since there is nothing obvious in the input to lead to the appropriate hypotheses, and the absence of certain error-types suggests that certain hypotheses are never, in fact, entertained. If L2 acquisition is a form of hypothesis-testing, then grammars underlying the L2 acquisition process will be essentially different from grammars internalized by native speakers. In other words, the L2 projection problem is actually denied, because the grammar is simply assumed not to contain the complex and abstract properties of the native speaker grammar. In that case, any deficiencies in the input are unimportant.

As long as one only considers unsuccessful L2 learners, hypothesis-testing looks relatively promising as an account of what takes place. But successful learners are a problem for hypothesis-testing models. If learners achieve knowledge of subtle and complex properties of language which are not present in the input, and which are not derivable from the mother tongue, a hypothesis-testing model simply has no way to account for this. The whole point of the UG claim is that these kinds of models fail for L1 acquisition. They also fail for L2 acquisition, when it is successful.

The situation comes down to this: if one assumes that UG does not operate and that L2 learning is a form of hypothesis-testing, the differences between L1 and L2 acquisition can be accounted for, particularly the lack of success of many L2 learners. However, there is then no adequate explanation of successful L2 acquisition in circumstances where UG-type knowledge could not have been obtained from the mother tongue. Alternatively, if one assumes that UG is present in L2 acquisition, this explains successful L2 acquisition, but leaves the failures still to be accounted for. It is possible that UG does operate and that the differences and difficulties can be attributed to other factors. Either way, one has something to explain. It is not the case that by assuming the non-operation of UG one has somehow explained a wider range of L2 acquisition phenomena than if one assumes UG still to be present.

2.6   UG and L2 acquisition: the alternatives

We are now in a position to consider some logical possibilities for a role for UG in L2 acquisition, and to discuss how one might decide between them. The major positions will be reviewed here. More detailed discussion of the experimental evidence will be reserved for later chapters. The following positions will be considered:

i.   UG is available and works exactly as it does in L1 acquisition.

ii.   UG is totally unavailable in L2 acquisition.

iii.   Access to UG is mediated via the L1. There are actually two different versions of this hypothesis:

a.   UG is inaccessible but any aspects of it available in the L1 can be used in the L2.

b.   L2 learners initially assume the L1 value of UG parameters, but are still able to tap UG. Hence, they can reset to L2 parameter settings.

iv. UG is available but does not work in identical fashion to L1 acquisition.

Although there are five positions listed here, these can be reduced to two main ones: the hypothesis that UG in some way or other plays a role in L2 acquisition (i, iiib and iv above), which I shall call the UG hypothesis, versus the hypothesis that UG is to all intents and purposes inaccessible (ii and iiia), which I shall call the UG-is-dead hypothesis.

2.6.1 *The pure UG hypothesis*

One possibility is that L1 and L2 acquisition are identical with respect to the operation of UG. On this view, L2 acquisition is assumed to be the result of a pure interaction between UG and the L2 data. The fact that the L2 learner already has knowledge of a language is considered irrelevant; there are assumed to be no effects from the mother tongue. This would be a UG-based equivalent of the creative construction model of Dulay and Burt (1974b), or of Krashen's theory of Acquisition (not Learning) (e.g. Krashen 1981). Although this is a logically possible position to hold, and it makes the strongest possible claim for the operation of UG, very few researchers working on UG in L2 acquisition subscribe to it.

2.6.2 *UG is dead*

An appealing possibility, in the light of the problems of many L2 learners and the differences between L1 and L2 acquisition discussed above, is that UG is no longer available to L2 learners, at least to adults (Clahsen and Muysken 1986; Schachter 1988b). Proponents of this view assume that the learning mechanisms underlying adult L2 acquisition are radically different from those underlying L1 acquisition, and that they are not unique to language, explaining the variation in degree of success in L2 acquisition as being similar to the variation in degree of success in other kinds of skill acquisition.

2.6.3 *Role of the L1*

There are two rather different positions on the role of the L1 in the UG literature. One is a version of the UG-is-dead position, which assumes that any mismatch between the L2 input and the L2 learner's grammar is mediated not by UG but by knowledge (including UG-type knowledge) derived from the L1 grammar (Bley-Vroman 1989; Clahsen and Muysken 1989; Schachter 1988a). On this view, UG is dead as an active force in L2 acquisition but aspects of it encoded in the L1 can still be tapped. This means that fixed principles exemplified in the L1, as well as L1 parameter settings, will be accessible to the L2 learner. However, since UG is no longer available as an active force, parameters of UG cannot be reset. If the L1 and the L2 differ as to the values they have for some parameter, the L2 value will not be attainable.

In contrast to this is a view which assumes a more active role for UG, but nevertheless attributes considerable importance to the L1 grammar. The L2 learner is assumed to be trying to arrive at a theory to deal with the L2 input; principles and parameter settings from the L1 are used, at least initially, as an interim theory about the L2 (Schwartz 1987; White 1986b, 1988b). The learner is not, however, assumed to be 'stuck' with L1 parameter settings; instead, parameter resetting to the L2 value is possible, on the basis of input from the L2 interacting with a still active UG.

2.6.4   *UG is partially available*

The idea that UG does not operate is attractive in that it offers a relatively simple explanation of the differences between L1 and L2 acquisition. The proponents of the UG-is-dead position (2.6.2) are adopting as their null hypothesis the assumption that L2 acquisition is not the same as L1. An alternative (2.6.1) is that L1 and L2 acquisition are identical. Both alternatives are misleading because of the implied binary contrast which fails to allow for the possibility that there are both similarities and differences between L1 and L2 acquisition. Once one allows for this, it is possible to consider the UG question in another way. That is, UG might be available but various factors might impinge on its operation. UG is only one component (one module) in an acquisition theory, whether of L1 or L2. This module will interact with various others and the failure of L2 learners (where they do fail) may be attributable to these other areas, and not necessarily to the non-operation of UG. A number of the differences between L1 and L2 acquisition can be accommodated within a theory of L2 acquisition that assumes that UG is still in some way available, without one's having to accept total identity of L1 and L2 acquisition.

2.7 Testing the issues: some general predictions

So far, we have arrived at the provisional conclusion that the UG hypothesis cannot be rejected out of hand, that a reasonable case can be made for the operation of UG in L2 acquisition, parallel to the case made in L1 acquisition. In order to consider this issue in depth, it is necessary to show that the UG hypothesis makes different predictions from the UG-is-dead hypothesis, since this will offer a means to choose between the two positions empirically. There are at least three areas in which the two positions make different predictions, and these areas are the focus of much of the research that will be discussed in subsequent chapters of this book.

2.7.1 UG effects

In L1 acquisition, there has now been considerable experimental investigation which suggests that the underlying competence of young children includes subtle and complex properties of language which are underdetermined by the input (for overview of the L1 acquisition evidence see Crain and Fodor, in press; Goodluck, in press). In other words, child grammars show effects which could only have come from UG.

The UG hypothesis makes the same kinds of predictions for L2 acquisition, i.e., that L2 learners should attain knowledge of ungrammaticality and ambiguity in the L2, and observe principles like Subjacency, the ECP, and the Binding Theory. In contrast, the UG-is-dead hypothesis predicts that L2 learners will not be able to attain this kind of knowledge (unless it is accessible through the L1), since this is precisely the sort of knowledge presumed to be unattainable via general learning strategies and hypothesis-testing. In order to show that UG is operating, then, it must be demonstrated that L2 learners possess the kind of unconscious knowledge that could only be obtained from UG, that their language use (comprehension and production) reflects UG effects.

2.7.2 No 'wild' grammars

Related to the issue of UG effects is the question of violations of principles of UG. Interim competence in L1 acquisition is usually assumed to be constrained by UG at all points (Goodluck 1986; Hyams 1986; Otsu 1981; Pinker 1984; White 1982). Goodluck (1986) refers to this as the 'no wild grammars' mandate; the assumption is that at no point in the course of language acquisition will the child come up with a grammar which violates UG.[6] For L1 acquisition, there has been some exploration of the question of whether learners produce violations of UG or interpret sentences in ways which are inconsistent with UG, and the evidence suggests that they are constrained by UG (e.g. Crain and Fodor, in press; Goodluck, in press). That is, there are certain error types that are predicted to be impossible if UG is in operation; these error types do indeed seem to be absent in child language.

Again, L2 acquisition should be similar. If the interlanguage grammars of L2 learners reflect the operation of UG at every point in the acquisition process, certain predictions arise with regard to the form of ILGs and the kinds of errors that L2 learners might make. ILGs should not contain rules of a kind prohibited by UG, and ILGs should not generate sentences which are violations of UG.

In this context, one can think of *impossible* errors. An impossible error would be one which indicated that the learner was violating some universal principle, suggesting that UG is not available. In other words, the error is impossible in the sense that it is prohibited by UG, not in the sense that it is logically impossible. For example, sentences like (4a) should not be produced by L2 learners, and *she* and *Mary* should not be interpreted coreferentially in sentences like (4b), since these would violate UG, and should therefore be impossible if UG is still operating.

(4) a. What does Mary believe the story that John saw?
     b. She watched television before Mary had dinner

If UG is dead, on the other hand, such UG violations might be expected to occur, as part of the hypothesis-testing process.

This does not, of course, mean that the UG hypothesis predicts no errors in L2 acquisition. Non-UG based errors will occur, such as (5):

(5) John run fast

There is no principle of UG which dictates that English requires 3rd-person singular agreement when the verb is in the present tense; this is a language-specific property of English which has to be learned. The fact that L2 learners have difficulty with this particular property and frequently produce forms like (5) is simply irrelevant to the UG question.

Other errors would also count as possible rather than impossible errors in the UG framework. Since parameters of UG are set differently for different languages, L2 learners might adopt an inappropriate parameter setting for the language being learned. In that case, forms might be produced which are ungrammatical in the target language but which are nevertheless permitted by UG, in that they are found in other languages (i.e., in those with the parameter setting in question). For example, a Spanish learner of English might produce a sentence like (6):

(6)   Is raining

(6) is ungrammatical in English, but its Spanish equivalent is grammatical. Hence, forms like (6) do not constitute violations of UG and are not evidence against the UG hypothesis.

2.7.3 *Tapping aspects of UG not exemplified in the L1*

A third area where the UG and the UG-is-dead hypotheses make different predictions concerns the accessibility of principles and parameter settings which are not exemplified in the L1. We have already seen that languages vary as to which principles and parameter settings they instantiate. Principles do not necessarily show up in all languages; for example, a principle like Subjacency, which is a constraint on movement, does not operate in languages without movement rules. Certain principles have parameters associated with them, with values which differ, as was the case with Head-position, discussed in Chapter 1.

The claim that the mother tongue grammar mediates L2 acquisition is consistent with either the presence or absence of UG in L2 acquisition (2.6.3). Indeed, where the L1 and the L2 both have the same principles operating, or the same values of parameters, it is impossible to distinguish between UG or the L1 grammar as the source of any complex UG-like knowledge. Thus, if the L1 and the L2 both observe Subjacency, or if they both show the head-initial setting of the Head-position Parameter, and if the L2 learner observes Subjacency in the L2 and assumes that it is head-initial, one cannot tell whether this was due to L1 knowledge or to the operation of UG.

However, there is a crucial difference in the two hypotheses for those cases where the L1 and L2 differ as to a principle or parameter setting. The UG-is-dead hypothesis predicts that L2 learners will only be able to tap aspects of UG exemplified in their L1s; they will neither be able to acquire a parameter value which is different from that of their L1 nor be able to activate a principle which was not operative in the L1. In contrast, the UG hypothesis predicts that parameter resetting is possible, and that principles not activated in the L1 can be tapped in the L2 acquisition context.

2.8 Conclusion

In this chapter, it has been suggested that there is a logical problem of L2 acquisition, and that a reasonable case can be made for a role for UG. Furthermore, the UG hypothesis is a testable one: it makes different empirical predictions from the UG-is-dead hypothesis. In subsequent chapters, we shall explore various versions of these two hypotheses, and consider the empirical evidence that researchers have brought to bear on the issue of UG in second language acquisition.

2.9 Further reading

i.   The interlanguage hypothesis is examined in detail by *Sharwood Smith* (to appear), who also discusses the role of UG in second language acquisition. *Gregg* (1989) discusses the importance of competence models in L2 acquisition research.

ii.   *Lightbown and White* (1988) provide a review of the influence of various linguistic theories on L1 and L2 acquisition research.

iii.   General arguments against UG in second language acquisition, based on differences between L1 and L2 acquisition, are to be found in *Bley-Vroman* (1989) and *Schachter* (1988b).

iv.   General arguments in favour of UG in second language acquisition are to be found in *Cook* (1985) and *White* (1985b, 1988b).

Notes to Chapter 2

1.   Of course, UG is not universally accepted as an explanation of L1 acquisition. However, there is no point in considering a role for UG in L2 acquisition unless one presupposes that it constrains L1 acquisition. All the theories discussed in this book agree that UG is involved in L1 acquisition; their differences centre on L2 acquisition.

2.   For further discussion of the competence/performance distinction in L2 acquisition, see Gregg (1989); Sharwood Smith, to appear.

3.   Assume that successful learners are those who achieve reasonable fluency and accuracy in their use of L2 syntax, such that their use of the L2 approximates fairly closely to that of a native speaker. This begs many questions but will serve for our current purposes.

4.   Ellis argues that the existence of negative evidence in L2 acquisition calls into question claims for UG in L1 acquisition. This is clearly absurd.

5.   Indeed, Schachter (1974) made this point very strongly, in her work on avoidance.

6.   However, there have been recent suggestions that some principles of UG emerge according to a maturational schedule (Borer and Wexler 1987). Any grammar formulated prior to the emergence of some principle may violate that principle (Felix 1984). Presumably, the maturational issue is irrelevant in the L2 acquisition context, since all principles will have matured in the course of L1 acquisition.

3 Testing for principles of Universal Grammar

3.1 Introduction

In this chapter, we shall discuss how to investigate empirically whether L2 acquisition is constrained by UG. In Chapter 1, a distinction was made between fixed principles, which apply in all languages that have the appropriate properties, and parameters, which allow for a limited range of variation between languages. Experimental evidence for and against the UG hypothesis will be reviewed in this chapter, particularly research that investigates principles which are not parameterized. As we shall see, the results do not offer a clear answer as to the availability or non-availability of UG.

3.2 Methodological considerations

3.2.1 *Tapping L2 competence*

Proponents of the UG hypothesis argue that L2 acquisition is constrained by UG. That is, the underlying competence of second language learners, at any stage of the acquisition process, should show evidence of the operation of universal principles. This raises the question of how one can establish whether this is in fact the case, and what methodologies are appropriate for experimental research into this question.

Linguistic competence is, of course, an abstraction, whether one is concerned with the competence of L1 or L2 learners, or of adult native speakers, or learners who have 'completed' the L2 acquisition process. It is also unconscious. There is no direct way to tap competence, but various aspects of linguistic performance can give insights into competence. Some aspects of performance are more revealing than others, and are amenable to experimental manipulation which can help in determining the nature of the L2 learner's underlying knowledge.

Where principles of UG are concerned, certain types of performance data cannot reveal enough to decide between the UG hypothesis and the UG-is-dead hypothesis. This is particularly true of spontaneous oral production data, whether cross-sectional or longitudinal. One might think that relevant production data could be found. They would consist of sentences which systematically violate principles of UG; these could be taken to indicate that UG does not constrain L2 acquisition, and thus support the UG-is-dead hypothesis. Absence of such data could indicate support for the UG hypothesis, since learners guided by UG should not violate universal principles. The problem is that a learner might fail by chance to produce structures which violate principles of UG; many of the relevant structures are fairly complex, as we have seen, and simply might not arise in the normal course of conversation, or during observation by an experimenter. (There is also the more practical question of how long one should wait before deciding that no violations are going to occur.) Therefore, absence of violations in spontaneous production does not allow us automatically to assume that UG is operating. Conversely, presence of violations does not necessarily mean that UG is unavailable; one needs to be sure that violations are systematic rather than random.[1]

Thus, it is necessary for the experimenter to be able to manipulate the sentence types to be investigated, rather than just relying on their chance occurrence in production data. Since linguistic competence includes knowledge of ungrammaticality, second language learners must somehow be made to reveal this knowledge, directly or indirectly. If they show that they do indeed find violations of UG to be ungrammatical, this lends support to the UG hypothesis.

One way of establishing whether L2 learners' competence includes knowledge that certain forms are impossible is by the use of grammaticality judgment (GJ) tasks, where learners are asked to judge the correctness or otherwise of various sentences. Many variants of GJ tasks are used in the experiments discussed in this book. An advantage of GJ tasks is that the experimenter can be sure that sentences which violate universal constraints are included for investigation. In this way, subjects are forced to consider whether a sentence which is 'impossible' from the point of view of UG is also impossible in their interlanguage.

There are a number of problems with GJ tasks, however, including the fact that subjects may show response biases (for example, they may show a tendency to accept all sentences, regardless of their grammaticality) and that they may be judging the sentences according to criteria which are not those intended by the experimenter (semantic criteria, rather than syntactic, for instance) (Birdsong 1989; Kellerman 1985). There are ways of alleviating these problems; most of the tests to be discussed in this chapter are designed in such a way that the operation of UG is only assumed if subjects respond accurately to both grammatical and ungrammatical sentences. Since these require the opposite responses (an acceptance of a grammatical sentence and a rejection of an ungrammatical one), successful performance is unlikely to be due to a response bias.

In many GJ tasks, it is possible to check whether subjects are judging the intended syntactic phenomenon by requiring them to supply corrections for sentences which they consider incorrect, or by asking for translations. However, in the case of the principles that will be considered in this chapter, this is rarely possible. When incorrect sentences violate abstract principles of UG, it is often hard for a native speaker, let alone a language learner, to work out what an appropriate correction would be.

One of Birdsong's objections to the use of GJ tasks in L2 acquisition research is that many learners may not have the metalinguistic skills necessary to perform such tasks, especially the illiterate or semi-literate, and that by using literate subjects one gets a very unrepresentative sample of L2 learners, and an inaccurate picture of L2 competence. This objection is not as serious as it seems. The fact that some learners may not be able to give metalinguistic judgments does not mean that judgment tasks should be altogether excluded. There are alternatives to GJ tasks as a means of tapping competence, which can be used with those who cannot make grammaticality judgments (and also with those that can). Researchers on L1 acquisition have long had to handle the problem of how to establish the competence of illiterate subjects (i.e., very young children). Just because they cannot use traditional, written, GJ tasks does not mean that one has to abandon the enterprise of determining what their competence consists of.

In L1 acquisition studies of linguistic competence, act-out tasks are often employed. The child is given a collection of toys. The experimenter utters a sentence and the child acts out his or her interpretation of the sentence with these toys. A similar procedure uses picture-identification, where the subject has to pick out which (if any) of a series of pictures best goes with the sentence uttered by the experimenter. Although such tasks often introduce additional processing difficulties, and pragmatic factors may conflict with the task requirements, they are a useful way of tapping interpretations of sentences, providing another way of determining linguistic competence. Surprisingly few UG-based L2 acquisition studies have adopted this sort of methodology (but see Flynn 1987b for the use of act-out tasks, and Finer and Broselow 1986 for the use of picture-identification).

There are other ways of getting subjects to manipulate L2 data, which allow insights into their unconscious knowledge of language. Some tasks follow the tradition in L2 acquisition research of taking avoidance behaviour as providing evidence about competence (Schachter 1974; Kleinmann 1978). Subjects are presented with sentences which must be combined or altered in such a way that a violation of UG would be a conceivable response. If subjects fail to violate UG in such circumstances, this is an indirect indication that they are constrained by universal principles.

When investigating whether L2 learners' competence is constrained by UG, it is also important to have native speaker control groups. If it turns out that L2 learners violate a principle of UG, one needs to be sure that this is because they are L2 learners. There are at least two other possibilities, both of which can be eliminated by use of control groups. The first possibility is that a particular task might lead to responses which violate UG, regardless of whether one is a language learner or a native speaker. The second is that theoretical linguists might make erroneous assumptions about native speaker competence; if native speakers behave as linguists expect, then any difference between them and L2 learners has to be taken seriously, but if the native speakers also violate principles of UG, it suggests that linguists may have incorrectly identified a principle of UG.

3.2.2 *Establishing appropriate levels of L2 proficiency*

Another point relevant to any experimental investigation of UG is the fact that a number of principles only apply in complex sentences, or to structures of a particular type. For example, Subjacency prevents movement over several bounding nodes (see 1.8.2.4), i.e., it is relevant to structures containing multiple clauses or complex NPs. This means that a learner who has not mastered a particular level of structure may not yet have the relevant principle operating in the grammar. The principle may not have been triggered. In a learner who has mastered only simple sentences, there is no need for a principle like Subjacency, but it should come into effect as soon as complex sentences and question formation are mastered.

When testing for the operation of UG, therefore, it is important that subjects are in fact able to handle the structures on which the principle being investigated would operate. Lack of sufficient knowledge of the L2 must be ruled out as a cause of problems; learners might violate a universal not because of the non-availability of UG, but because the structure in question is beyond their current capacity, and they are just stringing words together in an arbitrary fashion.

Otsu (1981) and White (1982) both point to this problem for L1 acquisition. It applies equally to L2 learners. In Otsu's empirical investigations of the L1 acquisition of linguistic universals, his solution is to include both a syntax test and a UG test, the former to test explicitly for whether the child has command of relevant structures and the latter to test for the presence or absence of principles of UG. Otsu and Naoi (1986) and Schachter (1988a, 1989b) use this methodology for L2 acquisition research as well. Other researchers achieve a similar effect by including grammatical sentences of equal complexity to the ungrammatical UG violations which are being tested (Bley-Vroman et al. 1988; White 1988a). The idea is that if subjects cannot perform accurately on the grammatical sentences, this indicates that they have not yet attained the structures in question, so it is inappropriate to look at the operation of UG with respect to these structures.

3.2.3 *Ruling out effects of the L1*

If UG operates in L2 acquisition, L2 learners should internalize knowledge that they could not have obtained from L2 input alone. Conversely, if UG is no longer available, they should not be able to work out properties of the L2 which are underdetermined by input data. This does not mean that one can simply investigate any principle of UG in order to determine whether it operates in second language acquisition. Principles like the Theta Criterion (1.8.2.2) and the Case Filter (1.8.2.5) appear to hold in all languages. If a particular principle operates in both the L1 and L2, and if it turns out that L2 learners observe this principle, this does not provide clear evidence for the operation of UG; it might just be due to transfer of L1 knowledge. The strongest arguments in favour of the operation of UG in L2 acquisition will be made in cases where effects of the L1 can be eliminated altogether.

A number of studies seek to rule out the possibility that the L1 provides the sole access to UG by choosing L1s and L2s that differ from each other in crucial respects. Recall that universal principles do not necessarily operate in all languages, but only in that subset of languages which exhibits the relevant properties; thus, a language without movement rules will not be subject to constraints on movement. If the L1 does not instantiate some principle but the L2 does, one can investigate whether L2 learners have access to UG independently of their L1. All the studies to be considered here are designed in this way; the L2 is English and the L1 is an oriental language like Japanese, Korean or Chinese. These languages differ from English in that they lack certain syntactic movement rules, so that universal principles relating to movement will presumably not have been triggered.[2] If native speakers of these languages reveal knowledge of constraints on movement in English, this suggests that UG must still be accessible to L2 learners.

Since certain properties of the above oriental languages are central to all of the studies to be discussed in this chapter, a brief overview will be given here, using examples from Japanese. The first property concerns the formation of *yes-no* questions. Japanese does not have a rule like the English subject-auxiliary inversion rule. Instead, questions are formed by adding an interrogative (Q) particle to the end of a declarative sentence, as can be seen in (1):[3]

(1)　a.　*Kore-wa hon desu*
　　　　this-TOP book is
　　　　'This is a book'
　　b.　*Kore-wa hon desu ka?*
　　　　this-TOP book is　Q particle
　　　　'Is this a book?'

The difference in the way Japanese and English form *yes-no* questions is relevant for the study by Otsu and Naoi (1986), where the lack of subject-auxiliary inversion in the first language and the need for it in the second are used to investigate whether L2 learners observe a universal principle known as Structure-Dependence.

The second property is that Japanese is a rigidly verb final language; nothing can move to the right of the verb, in contrast to English which has rules of extraposition to the right. Ritchie's (1978) study makes use of this difference to investigate whether or not Japanese learners of English observe constraints on rightward movement.

The third property of Japanese (shared by Korean and Chinese) is that *wh*-questions are formed without *wh*-movement. The *wh*-word stays in its deep structure position, rather than moving to the front of the clause or sentence as it would in English. In (2), the *wh*-word *dare* stays in the direct object (DO) position:[4]

(2)　a.　*John-wa　dare-o　korosita　ka*
　　　　John-TOP　who-DO　killed　　　Q particle
　　　　'Who did John kill?'

　　b.　*John-wa　Mary-ga　　dare-o　kiratte-iru　to*
　　　　John-TOP　Mary-particle　who-DO　hating-is　　that
　　　　sinzite-ita　　ka?
　　　　believing-was　Q particle
　　　　'Who did John believe that Mary hated?'

As can be seen in (2b), *wh*-words are not extracted from embedded clauses to form questions. It is precisely in the case of such extractions in languages like English that Subjacency becomes relevant, preventing certain kinds of extractions and allowing others. The assumption that Subjacency does not operate in languages like Japanese but does operate in English is important in the work of Schachter (1988a, 1989b) and Bley-Vroman et al. (1988).

Wh-movement in languages like English leaves a trace behind, to mark the site of the moved *wh*-word. This trace is subject to the Empty Category Principle (ECP) (1.8.2.8). In languages like Japanese and Korean, since the *wh*-word remains in its deep structure position, there will be no trace and hence the ECP will not be relevant. Bley-Vroman et al. (1988) look at whether the ECP operates in the English L2 of native speakers of Korean.

3.3　Experimental studies on principles of UG

3.3.1　*Structure-Dependence*

A small study by Otsu and Naoi (1986) looks at the principle of Structure-Dependence (Chomsky 1975). Structure-Dependence says that linguistic rules must operate on structural units, rather than on linear concepts like first word, second word, or last word. This explains why (3c) could not be the question version of (3a):

(3)   a.   The boy who is standing over there is happy
      b.   Is the boy who is standing over there _ happy?
      c.   *Is the boy who _ standing over there is happy?

The question formation rule must be formulated in terms of some structural concept like *subject*, so that when the subject of the sentence is a complex NP including a relative clause, this whole complex is treated as a unit, as is the case with the correctly formed question (3b). Questions are not formed by moving the first verb to the front of the sentence, as in (3c), even though this would be a logical possibility.

Otsu and Naoi look at whether L2 learners' hypotheses about the L2 are structure-dependent, as would be predicted if L2 acquisition is guided by UG. Subjects were Japanese-speaking learners of English. At issue is whether they will correctly form questions when the subject of the sentence includes a relative clause. The formation of such questions in Japanese provides no clue as to how it is done in English. As mentioned in 3.2.3, *yes-no* questions are formed by the addition of a question particle to a declarative sentence, with no change in word order. If learners try to extract generalizations from the L2 input without UG to guide them, a perfectly reasonable hypothesis is the one that is structure-independent and incorrect, namely that the first verb in the sentence is moved to the front. This is a hypothesis which is consistent with question formation in simple sentences; one can only distinguish between this and the correct, structure-dependent, rule by looking at structures like those in (3), where the two ways of forming questions yield different results. Otsu and Naoi are interested in whether their subjects will produce incorrect questions like (3c) or correct ones like (3b). If the latter are exclusively or predominantly produced, it suggests that Japanese-speaking learners are guided by the principle of Structure-Dependence, in spite of the fact that it is not relevant to these structures in their mother tongue.

Subjects were eleven females in Grade 9 (ages 14-15), who had studied English for two years, both at school and in a special after-school programme. Crucially, at the time of testing they had not yet been taught relative clauses. They had, however, been taught how to form questions in simple sentences. Subjects received a training session introducing them to English relative clauses in sentence types different from those used in the actual testing. Testing consisted of two parts: (a) a syntax test to determine whether subjects had mastered the relative clause structure, and (b) a question formation task to determine whether Structure-Dependence was observed or not.

As discussed above, there is no point in testing for a universal principle if subjects have not mastered the kinds of structures in which that principle would operate. Otsu and Naoi's design is intended to eliminate from consideration any students who have not yet mastered relative clauses.[5] The design is presented schematically in Figure 3.1.

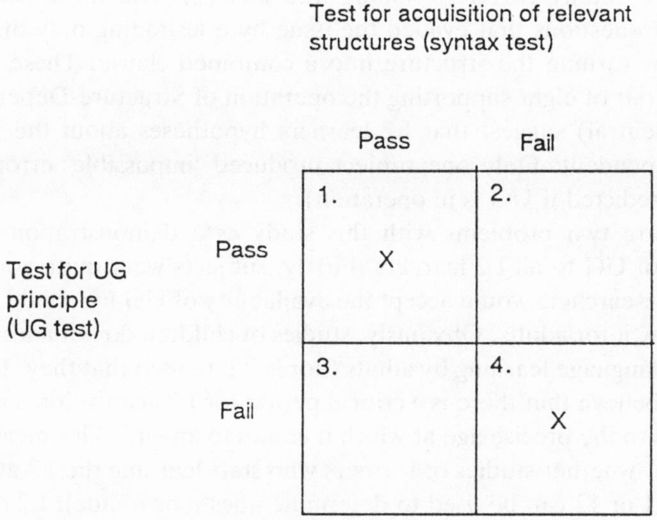

Test for acquisition of relevant
structures (syntax test)

		Pass	Fail
Test for UG principle (UG test)	Pass	1. X	2.
	Fail	3.	4. X

Figure 3.1 Research design for testing for UG

The predictions resulting from this design are as follows: subjects who pass the test for the acquisition of relevant structures (the syntax test) are expected to pass the UG test, showing evidence of observing the appropriate UG principle; these subjects will fall into box 1. Subjects who fail the syntax test are not expected to observe the principle, falling into box 4. Subjects falling into boxes (2) and (3) would be potential counter-examples to the hypothesis that UG operates in L2 acquisition.[6]

In Otsu and Naoi's study, the syntax test required translation of declarative sentences with relative clauses from Japanese to English. For the UG test, subjects had to transform twelve English declarative sentences into interrogatives. Of these twelve, four were distractors and eight were like (4):

(4)   The girl that is smiling can jump high

All subjects passed the syntax test, suggesting that they could handle the structure of relative clauses. In the UG test, only one subject produced responses which did not observe Structure-Dependence. This subject produced questions like (5) for five of the eight test sentences:

(5)   Is the girl that smiling can jump high?

This subject would fall into box (3) of Figure 3.1. Seven subjects produced the questions totally correctly, falling into box (1), and three produced grammatical questions that evaded the issue by questioning only the main clause, or by turning the structure into a conjoined clause. These results (with seven out of eight supporting the operation of Structure-Dependence and three neutral) suggest that L2 learners hypotheses about the L2 are structure-dependent. Only one subject produced 'impossible' errors (i.e. forms not predicted if UG is in operation).

There are two problems with this study as a demonstration of the availability of UG to all L2 learners. Firstly, subjects were quite young. A number of researchers would accept the availability of UG for child L2 learners but deny it for adults. Obviously, studies of children do not address the question of language learning by adults (nor is it intended that they should). Those who believe that there is a critical period for L2 acquisition are often uncertain as to the precise age at which it comes to an end. This means that it is not clear whether studies of learners who start learning the L2 at about the age of 11 or 12 can be used to determine questions of adult L2 competence — it depends whether or not one believes the critical period to be over by this age.

Secondly, although Structure-Dependence plays no role in question formation of this type in Japanese, it presumably does constrain other structures in Japanese. It might be that Otsu and Naoi's subjects tapped knowledge of Structure-Dependence via other structures in their L1, and were applying L1-based knowledge of this principle to new structures in the L2. In other words, this is not, after all, a clear case of a principle which does not operate in the L1. As we shall see, this problem affects other studies to be discussed in this chapter.

3.3.2. *The Right Roof Constraint*

Ritchie (1978) is specifically interested in the issue of whether UG is available to adult learners. He also investigates a principle which does not, apparently, operate in the L1 at all, but is required in the L2, thus in principle eliminating the possibility that UG-type knowledge is simply transferred by adult learners from their L1.

Once again, the L1 in question is Japanese, a strictly verb final language, which has no rightward movement rules. The L2 is English, which does allow rightward movement, or *extraposition*, subject to certain bounding conditions (Ross 1967; Baltin 1981). Constraints on rightward movement, then, will not have been activated in the L1 Japanese, so L1 knowledge cannot mediate L2 performance. Therefore, if adult learners of English whose mother tongue is Japanese show evidence of observing bounding conditions on rightward movement, this suggests that UG still operates, that principles are still accessible by them, on the assumption that there would be no other way of attaining this knowledge.

The specific principle Ritchie looked at is called the Right Roof Constraint (RRC). (6b) and (7b) are some examples of possible rightward movement in English, where a PP modifier has been extracted from its NP. The versions without rightward movement are given in (6a) and (7a). Although rightward movement is possible in English, a phrase cannot move freely anywhere to the right, as can be seen by the ungrammaticality of (7c):[7]

(6) a.   [A book by Chomsky] has just come out
     b.   [A book _] has just come out by Chomsky
(7) a.   That [a book by Chomsky] has just come out is not surprising
     b.   That [a book _] has just come out by Chomsky is not surprising
     c.   *That [a book _] has just come out is not surprising by Chomsky

The RRC disallows sentences like (7c); roughly speaking, it says that an element may not move to the right out of the clause in which it originated. This is a stricter requirement than leftward movement, where phrases can move out of the clause in which they originate. If learners decided to use leftward movement as some sort of guide as to how to proceed with rightward movement in English, they should go wrong.

Ritchie's subjects were twenty adult Japanese graduate students and faculty at an American university, who were quite advanced in their knowledge of English. There were six native speakers to serve as a control group.

The test was a questionnaire consisting of 120 sentence pairs. Subjects had to compare sentences and judge them against each other. For example, subjects were presented with sentences like (7b) and (7c) and asked to indicate whether (b) was more grammatical than (c) or vice versa, or whether they were the same. The idea of comparing sentences is a good one; it means that subjects do not have to make outright judgments, which are often affected by extraneous factors like vocabulary choice.

The vast majority of sentence pairs in the test are not directly relevant for the RRC. They were included to check the following: that subjects can do this kind of task, that they have command of the relevant vocabulary and structural complexity, that they are not basing their judgments on sentence length. In other words, implicit in his design is the idea that is explicit in that of Otsu and Naoi, namely to make sure that the subjects have mastered the structures on which the constraint would be expected to operate. However, in many of Ritchie's sentence pairs, one of the sentences is semantically anomalous but syntactically correct.[8] It is not clear what the rationale for these sentences is; using semantic anomalies does not appear to be an appropriate way of establishing syntactic competence, and may well have influenced the results in unexpected ways.[9] None of the test sentence pairs, that is those testing for violations of the RRC, included semantic anomalies, however.

The results fairly strongly suggest that RRC is operating. Ritchie's study included two different extraposition structures. In the case of one of them, the judgments of sixteen out of twenty subjects suggest that the RRC is being observed (and the other four do not show violations of RRC); in the case of the other, thirteen observe the RRC, two violate it, and five are neutral.

Although Ritchie argues, on the basis of these results, that adult learners have access to UG, this conclusion is in fact too strong. Most of the subjects had been taught English at school in Japan from the age of 13, and in a few cases younger, so they were not true adult learners.

3.3.3 *Subjacency and the Empty Category Principle*

3.3.3.1 *Schachter*
The logic that underlies the two previous experiments, namely that the UG hypothesis would be supported if the L2 learner acquires properties of the L2 which are not obvious from the L2 input and which are not derivable

from the L1, is also adopted by Schachter (1988a, 1989b). Unlike the cases cited above, her evidence suggests that principles of UG are only observed in L2 acquisition when they operate in a similar fashion in the L1 and the L2, in other words, that UG can only be accessed via the L1.

The principle that Schachter looks at is Subjacency, a constraint on syntactic movement rules. As we saw in Chapter 1, Subjacency says that elements cannot move over more than one bounding node in a single operation. This explains the ungrammaticality of sentences like (8) in English, where the *wh*-element has moved over too many bounding nodes:

(8)   a.   *Who$_i$ [do you believe [the claim [that John saw t$_i$]]]?
       b.   *Who$_i$ [do you wonder [whether [John will visit t$_i$]]]?

Languages which have movement rules must observe Subjacency. In languages without overt *wh*-movement, Subjacency does not apply (or at least not in *wh*-structures).

Schachter's (1989b) subjects are native speakers of Indonesian, Korean and Chinese learning English. Korean, like Japanese, is a language without *wh*-movement; in *wh*-questions, the *wh* word remains in its deep structure position, as in (2) above. Since Subjacency is a constraint on movement at surface structure, Schachter's assumption is that Korean-speakers will not have had the exposure to Subjacency in the L1. Although Chinese has no *wh*-movement, there are other movement operations which appear to be subject to Subjacency (Huang 1982), so that the Chinese-speakers may have had exposure to Subjacency in the L1, but not in *wh*-questions. According to Schachter, Indonesian has *wh*-movement but it is more limited than in English; where *wh*-movement occurs, it observes Subjacency.[10] Schachter (1988a) adds a group of native-speakers of Dutch; Dutch is very similar to English with respect to *wh*-movement and Subjacency.

Thus, Schachter can test whether UG is activatable for adults whose L1 does not show a constraint (Korean) or whether it can only be activated if it is already available in the L1 (Dutch), or whether it cannot be activated at all. The Chinese and Indonesians provide an interesting intermediate case: Subjacency is activated in the L1 but not in the same range of structures as in the L2. If UG is actually dead and only accessible via the L1, such learners should not be able to apply Subjacency to new situations in the L2.

Schachter (independently) arrived at a design almost identical to that of Otsu (1981) and Otsu and Naoi (1986). She uses a grammaticality judgment task. For each sentence to be judged, subjects are asked to indicate whether they think it is clearly grammatical, probably grammatical, probably not grammatical, or not grammatical. The test includes grammatical sentences designed to ensure that subjects have reached a level at which Subjacency should have emerged in the L2; these constitute the syntax test. The ungrammatical sentences are Subjacency violations; these constitute the Subjacency test (or UG test). The syntax test sentences were 24 grammatical sentences with the following structures: sentential subjects, relative clauses, noun phrase complements and embedded questions. There were an equal number of sentences testing Subjacency, with extractions out of these same structures, i.e., sentences that are ungrammatical in English. For example, (9a) is one of her grammatical relative clause sentences, while (9b) is an ungrammatical extraction from a relative clause, a Subjacency violation:

(9)   a.   The theory we discussed yesterday will be on the exam next week.
      b.   What did Susan visit the store that had in stock?

Schachter makes the same predictions as Otsu and Naoi (1986), namely that if L2 learners can still access UG, they should pass both the syntax test and the Subjacency test. Those who fail both tests would simply not yet have sufficient knowledge of the structures in question for Subjacency to be in operation. Any subjects who pass the syntax test but not the Subjacency test, or vice versa, would constitute evidence against the UG hypothesis.

It is worth reiterating that this design allows one to reduce the effects of response biases as an explanation of successful or totally unsuccessful performance. In order to succeed at both the syntax test and the Subjacency test, subjects must accept grammatical sentences and reject ungrammatical ones. In order to fail at both the syntax test and the Subjacency test, subjects must reject the grammatical sentences and accept ungrammatical ones. Thus a bias towards accepting or rejecting all sentences will not cause subjects to fall into either of the boxes 1 and 4 of Figure 3.1. However, such biases could cause subjects to fall into box 2 (if they have a tendency to reject all sentences) or box 3 (if they have a tendency to accept all sentences).

Schachter's subjects were all highly proficient in English; there were twenty Chinese-speakers, twenty one Korean-speakers, twenty Indonesian-speakers, eighteen Dutch-speakers, and nineteen native speaker controls. Their mean ages on first starting to learn English were 13.9 for the Chinese, 15.2 for the Koreans, 12.2 for the Indonesians, and 11.7 for the Dutch. Schachter assumes that all of these subjects should count as post-critical period learners, though one might question this assumption, particularly in the case of the native speakers of Dutch. It is also likely that the Dutch-speakers would have had much more exposure to English during their school years than the other groups. This means that the Dutch-speaking subjects may have had advantages when compared to the other groups, over and above the fact that their language observes Subjacency.

Schachter found that the native speaker controls performed as predicted, being very accurate both on the grammatical sentences and on the ungrammatical Subjacency violations. Only the Dutch-speaking subjects achieved scores like the native speakers. The native speakers of Chinese, Korean, and Indonesian were quite accurate on the grammatical sentences but many of them failed to reject Subjacency violations. In other words, they passed the syntax test but failed the Subjacency test, falling into box 3 of Figure 3.1. The overall results are given in Table 3.1.[11]

Table 3.1   Mean scores on grammatical and ungrammatical sentences (Schachter 1988a)

	Grammatical (n=24)	Ungrammatical (n=24)
Controls	21.6	21.2
Dutch	22.2	21.9
Indonesian	21.1	15.2
Chinese	21.1	17.2
Korean	19.8	12.4

These results indicate that where a principle operates in a similar fashion in both the L1 and L2, it can still be accessed by the L2 learner.[12] The Dutch-speaking subjects perform with considerable accuracy, just like native speakers. Where the L1 does not exemplify a principle, Schachter suggests that it cannot be accessed in the L2, explaining the poor performance of the Korean-speakers as far as ungrammatical Subjacency violations are concerned. They appear to be operating at chance on these sentences. Where the L1 uses a principle but not in the same range of structures as the L2, there appears to be partial access to the principle, as indicated in the results of the speakers of Chinese and Indonesian, who fall between the Dutch and the Koreans, achieving better than chance accuracy on the Subjacency violations.

Within the UG framework, we have been considering two possibilities as far as a role for the L1 is concerned. One is that UG is effectively unavailable (dead), but that principles exemplified in the L1 can still be accessed. On this view, principles not activated in the L1, and parameter settings different from those of the L1, cannot be accessed. The alternative position is that UG is still an active force. Although the L1 may provide an initial theory as to what the L2 is like, positive evidence in the L2 should be able to trigger principles that have not been instantiated in the L1. Schachter's results appear to support the former of these two positions; Subjacency did not seem to have been triggered for the Korean-speakers on the basis of exposure to *wh*-movement in English. Furthermore, all experimental groups except the Dutch-speakers accepted Subjacency violations, suggesting that their grammars were not constrained by UG.

However, there are a number of alternative explanations of these results which need to be considered before rejecting a role for UG in L2 acquisition. Firstly, methodological considerations may be partially responsible for the failure of so many of the subjects to reject Subjacency violations. Recall that the rationale for a syntax test is to ensure that subjects have mastered the structures in which Subjacency is expected to operate. Because the native speakers almost exclusively accept the grammatical syntax test sentences and reject the ungrammatical Subjacency violations, Schachter assumes that her syntax test sentences are indeed an appropriate test of whether learners have reached a level where Subjacency would be expected to operate. In fact, this is not necessarily the case. The native speakers of English would probably have accepted any grammatical sentences and rejected any ungrammatical ones, even if there was **no** relationship between the two. Thus, while I agree with Schachter that it is essential to have a syntax test, the native speaker judgments are not a guarantee that one has the right syntax test. Schachter's syntax test sentences and UG test sentences were not controlled for length and vocabulary choice, and were only partially comparable in terms of syntactic structure. The fact that the native speakers of Dutch behaved like the native speakers of English may have been due to the fact that they were more advanced in their English than the other subjects, rather than to the fact that only they had access to Subjacency.[13]

Two interesting theoretical possibilities can also account for the failure of the speakers of Indonesian, Chinese, and Korean to reject Subjacency violations. One is that Subjacency is in fact subject to parametric variation. Rizzi (1982) and Sportiche (1981) have argued that Italian and French, respectively, differ from English with respect to bounding nodes for Subjacency. Like English, these languages have movement and therefore observe Subjacency, but S is not a bounding node in these languages. In consequence, certain cases of extraction from *wh*-islands and noun complements are possible which are not possible in English. Some of the ungrammatical Subjacency violations used as test sentences by Schachter would not be violations in languages which have different bounding nodes from English. One possibility, then, is that subjects might have the been observing Subjacency but not the appropriate bounding nodes for English. (See 4.7 for further discussion of parameterized bounding nodes for Subjacency, and 6.4 for other cases where L2 learners pick inappropriate parameter values for the L2.)

The second possibility is advanced by Martohardjono and Gair (1989). Current analyses of languages like Indonesian, Chinese, Korean and Japanese assume an empty category *pro* (1.8.2.8). This category is not the result of movement but is base-generated. Martohardjono and Gair suggest that native speakers of oriental languages do not attribute a movement structure to *wh*-questions in the L2, but rather assume the presence of this *pro* in English, as in (10):

(10) a. Who [do you believe [the claim [that John saw *pro*]]]?
      b. Who [do you wonder [whether [John will visit *pro*]]]?

As a result, Subjacency is not involved, since Subjacency constrains movement but not the occurrence base-generated *pro*. Thus, the acceptance of Subjacency violations in the L2 is not an indication of the non-availability of a principle of UG but, rather, of an analysis of the L2 (stemming from the L1) in which Subjacency is simply irrelevant. Since Dutch, like English, does not have the empty category *pro*, the Dutch-speaking subjects would not be misled into misanalyzing English in this way, and correctly observe Subjacency. In support of their hypothesis, Martohardjono and Gair present data from Indonesian learners of English which suggest that a variety of syntactic phenomena (independent of the Subjacency issue) cluster in the ILG, and can all be attributed to the *pro* analysis.

3.3.3.2 *Bley-Vroman et al.*

So far, we have considered studies which suggest that UG is available to L2 learners (Otsu and Naoi 1986; Ritchie 1978) and studies which suggest that it is only weakly available, via the L1 (Schachter 1988a, 1989b). We turn now to a study whose results fall somewhere in between those discussed so far. Bley-Vroman, Felix and Ioup (1988) are also interested in the question of whether principles of UG are available to adult learners. Once again, the L2, English, has syntactic movement and the L1, Korean, does not. In this study, Subjacency is investigated, along with another principle of grammar that applies in the case of *wh*-movement, namely the ECP (1.8.2.8). The logic is the same as in the studies discussed above. If the L2 learner demonstrates knowledge of Subjacency, which could not have been obtained from the L1, and which is not obviously inferable from the L2 input, then this suggests that UG must be available to adult L2 learners. The situation regarding the ECP is slightly different. Languages without syntactic movement, like Korean and Japanese, nevertheless have movement at the level of Logical Form (LF) (1.8.1), and traces must be properly governed at LF. In other words, the ECP operates in Korean, but would never have applied to syntactic *wh*-movement structures, since these do not exist. It is possible that Korean-speaking learners of English might have access to the ECP but not to Subjacency, if UG is only accessible via the L1.

Subjects were 92 adult Korean-speakers, who were at an advanced level of English proficiency. They had initially learned English in Korea (presumably starting in their teens) but had spent, on average, over 3 years in the USA. There was a control group of 34 native speakers of English.

The test was a grammaticality judgment task, with 32 *wh*-movement sentences, approximately half of which were ungrammatical.[14] These ungrammatical sentences violated Subjacency or the ECP. The desire to find out whether L2 learners observe general principles of UG can lead to problems when these principles encompass a range of syntactic phenomena, as is the case with Subjacency and the ECP, which constrain movement out of a number of different structures. This means that tests for the operation of such principles often make use of many different sentence types, and there is a danger of having insufficient exemplars of each of the different types. The study by Bley-Vroman et al. suffers here; some of the structural categories that they look at have only one test sentence. Schachter's study is much better in this respect, since she takes care to have an equal number of sentences for each subcategory that she is interested in.

Subjects were asked to indicate whether a sentence was possible or impossible in English, or whether they were uncertain. There were very few responses of the latter type. Subjects were assigned a score which reflects the percentage of correctly accepted grammatical sentences and correctly rejected ungrammatical ones, in other words, an accuracy score. The average score of the control group was 92%; that of the experimental subjects was significantly lower, at 75%, but significantly higher than chance. However, the Korean-speakers were significantly better at rejecting ungrammatical examples (81%) than at accepting grammatical ones (68%), suggesting a response bias towards rejecting sentences. The Korean-speakers did not perform any worse on Subjacency violations than on ECP violations, suggesting that when a principle operates at a different level in the L1 (as is the case with the ECP), this does not give the learner more of an advantage than when the principle does not operate at all in the L1 (as is the case with Subjacency).

The results from various sentences were also analyzed in a way which is similar to that presented in Figure 3.1. That is, a grammatical *wh*-movement sentence and its ungrammatical equivalent are considered as the syntax test and the UG test respectively. Native speakers fall largely into box 1, that is for almost all the sentences paired in this way, they accept the grammatical and reject the ungrammatical. Only slightly over half of the Korean-speakers, on the other hand, give this kind of response. This is nevertheless considerably greater than chance accuracy: given that there are four possible cells into which they could fall, chance performance would be 25%. Over 20% of non-native responses fall into box 2, indicating that both the grammatical and the ungrammatical sentence were rejected, again suggesting a tendency to reject all sentences.[15]

Both these ways of analyzing the data reveal that subjects achieve scores considerably higher than chance. This is unexpected if UG is no longer available. On the other hand, if UG is still available, one might expect even greater accuracy, i.e. closer to the native speakers. Grimshaw and Rosen (in press) discuss similar discrepancies in the L1 acquisition research. They point out that if language learners show greater than chance knowledge of a principle of UG, and if there is no other way they could have arrived at this knowledge, one must assume that the principle is in fact available to learners and that other factors sometimes lead them to override the principles in performance. Although they make these remarks with respect to L1 acquisition, they are equally applicable to L2.

3.4 Recurring problems

Several issues have arisen which are common to the studies in this chapter, and which raise problems when trying to investigate whether UG plays a role in L2 acquisition. One is the changing nature of linguistic theory. Theoretical linguists are constantly refining and altering their views of the precise properties of UG. This is inevitable and is a healthy sign of theory development. However, it does pose problems for L2 acquisition research, in that the effects of principles may turn out to be somewhat different from what was originally assumed, or a principle may operate far more widely than was originally assumed. This is the case with Subjacency. Schachter (1988a, 1989b) and Bley-Vroman et al. (1988) assume that Subjacency does not operate in languages like Korean and Japanese; this is essential to their research design because they are attempting to isolate a principle which operates in the L2 but not the L1. However, Saito (1985) argues that Subjacency does operate in Japanese, though not in *wh*-structures. If this is correct, then the situation with Subjacency is similar to the one regarding Structure-Dependence. It operates, but in a different range of structures, so that one cannot totally exclude L1 knowledge after all. This problem also affects the RRC, though perhaps not seriously. Constraints on rightward movement are now subsumed under Subjacency, although this operates more strictly than it does when constraining leftward movement (Baltin 1981). If Subjacency is after all available in the L1 Korean or Japanese, it might be argued that this is what gives Ritchie's subjects knowledge of constraints on rightward movement in English. However, since rightward movement is even tighter than Subjacency normally requires, and since there is no rightward movement in Japanese, it is still not clear that the L1 could have provided this knowledge about English to Ritchie's subjects.

A related issue is raised by principles which operate at different levels in L1 and L2, e.g., the ECP operating at S-structure and LF in English but only at LF in Korean, Japanese and Chinese. Such possibilities make it difficult to tease apart the UG hypothesis from the UG-is-dead hypothesis. If an L2 learner appears to be following a principle of UG which turns out to operate in the L1, although at a different syntactic level, it makes it harder to rule out L1 transfer as the source of UG-like knowledge. Nevertheless, one can make a number of working hypotheses (which can themselves be tested) to handle this kind of situation; for example, one might assume that principles which operate at LF in the L1 cannot be used to determine properties of S-structure in the L2.

3.5 Conclusion

The experiments reported in this chapter offer conflicting evidence on the status of UG in L2 acquisition. Schachter's study suggests that only when a principle is activated in the L1 can it be readily accessed in the L2. In contrast, the studies by Otsu and Naoi (1986) and by Ritchie (1978) suggest that principles which are not exemplified in the L1 can be activated in the L2. Learners appear to be able to go beyond the L2 input and do not, on the whole, accept or produce 'impossible' errors. The Bley-Vroman et al. study suggests that L2 learners do considerably better than chance and hence that UG must be accessible in some form, even when the principles are not instantiated in the L1. However, indirect effects from the L1 cannot be totally ruled out in most of these cases, contrary to the researchers' original assumptions. Differences in methodology are probably partially responsible for these differences in the results. Clearly, the issue of whether UG operates in L2 acquisition has not yet been satisfactorily resolved. More rigorous studies are required, which adopt the logic of those discussed here in trying to rule out effects of the L1, and which make use of subjects who genuinely began their second language acquisition as adults.

3.6 Further reading

A number of the papers in *Flynn and O'Neil* (1988) investigate whether L2 learners have access to the principles that have been discussed in this chapter. Some of these look at cases where the L1 and L2 share a principle e.g. *White*'s paper on Subjacency and the ECP in French learners of English. Others follow the logic of this chapter and look at the case where the L1 and L2 differ with respect to the operation of principles e.g. *Felix*'s paper on the acquisition of English by native speakers of German.

Notes to Chapter 3

1. In the case of parameters, on the other hand, spontaneous production errors can be quite revealing. This issue will be discussed further in Chapter 4.

2. They do, however, allow fairly free permutations of word order known as *scrambling*.

3. These examples come from Kuno (1973).

4.   Japanese is an SOV language. Direct objects and clauses which are complements to the verb precede the verb.

5.   See Otsu (1981) for more details. Schachter (1989b) independently makes the same assumptions and arrives at the same kind of research design.

6.   Actually, it is not entirely clear that this is so. It is conceivable that subjects might fall into box 2 if they did not really understand the structures involved but the principles were powerful enough to operate in any case. Such an assumption underlies Felix's (1988) analysis of his results where he found that subjects were much more accurate on ungrammatical UG violations than on grammatical sentences. (Alternatively, as suggested by Birdsong 1989, this could be the effect of a response bias towards saying that everything is ungrammatical.) In L1 acquisition at least, box (3) is potentially explicable, on the hypothesis that certain principles of UG mature after others, but I assume that maturation of principles cannot be involved in L2 acquisition.

7.   Sentences like (7b) with rightward movement can be quite awkward in English, and many of Ritchie's examples are very cumbersome. However, the important thing is the contrast between these awkward but grammatical sentences, and the totally ungrammatical ones, like (7c).

8.   For example, *John had climbed a letter*.

9.   See Schachter (1989a) for criticisms of Ritchie's study.

10.   However, this analysis of Indonesian is questioned by Martohardjono and Gair (1989).

11.   This table is adapted from Schachter (1988a). More detailed breakdown of the results is given in Schachter (1989b).

12.   Similar results are reported by White (1988a). When the L1 is French, a language which observes Subjacency, and the L2 is English, learners observe Subjacency in the L2. Differences in bounding nodes between French and English, however, have some effects. See Chapter 4 for further discussion.

13.   Schachter does not provide an independent measure of ESL level to compare the Dutch-speaking subjects to the others. Independent measures for the Koreans, Indonesians and Chinese, on the other hand, were available, which showed them to be at comparable levels.

14.   This contrasts with Schachter, who mainly used structures without *wh*-movement as her grammatical sentences.

15.   Note that this is the opposite of Schachter's results, where the tendency for those who are not accurate on both types is to accept sentences.

4.1 Conceptual issues

We turn now to the role of parameters of UG in L2 acquisition. In Chapter 1, we saw that certain principles vary in their operation from language to language; this variation is built into UG in the form of parameters with different settings. If UG still operates in L2 acquisition, then parameters can be expected to have effects, though not necessarily the same kinds of effects as non-parameterized principles. In this chapter, we shall consider cases where a given parameter is set differently in the L1 and the L2. In such situations language transfer may occur, in the form of the initial transfer of the L1 parameter setting onto the L2.

Before looking at the implications of parameter theory for L2 acquisition, a potential conceptual problem must be considered. What does it mean for UG to be set in two different ways at once, one way for the L1 and another for the L2? This is a problem which does not arise in the context of other principles. As discussed in the previous chapter, principles which are not parameterized either operate in both languages, or do not operate in one of them because structural properties of the language are such that the principle is irrelevant. Thus, there is no potential contradiction. In the case of parameterized principles, on the other hand, there will be situations where a parameter seems to exhibit contradictory settings.

Chomsky (1986) suggests that certain idealizations are necessary, in particular the assumption of a homogeneous speech community, in order to be able to develop parameter theory as an account of L1 acquisition:

> The language of the hypothesized speech community.... is taken to be a 'pure' instance of UG ... We exclude, for example, a speech community of uniform speakers, each of whom speaks a mixture of Russian and French

..... The language of such a community would not be 'pure' in the relevant
sense, because it would not represent a single set of choices among the
options permitted by UG but rather would include 'contradictory' choices
for certain of these options. (p.17)

Is this a problem in the L2 acquisition context? If Chomsky means that
a 'mixture' of languages is to be represented by one grammar, then certainly, contradictory choices for parameters will arise. However, it is not
clear that this is in fact the appropriate way to represent knowledge of more
than one language. Presumably, there will be two grammars, one for each
language. If we think of L2 acquisition as leading to the internalizing of a
separate grammar for the L2, the standard assumption in most versions of
the interlanguage hypothesis, then contradictory choices do not arise after
all. A parameter may be set one way for one language and a different way
for another language; two different grammars are involved here, not one
grammar with contradictory settings. Thus, when researchers speak of
parameter *resetting* in second language acquisition, the idea is not that L2
learners have to lose the L1 parameter setting for the L1. Rather, if their
initial assumption for the L2 was that the L1 setting was appropriate, this
has to be reset for the L2, while the original setting is maintained for the
L1.

4.2 The role of the L1 parameter setting

In Chapter 2, several positions on UG in second language acquisition were
outlined. In this chapter, the main focus will be on claims that the L1
parameter setting has effects in L2 acquisition. As we have already seen,
the view that the L2 learner adopts L1 parameter settings is actually consistent with two very different assumptions about UG, namely the assumption
that UG is still available as an active force and the assumption that it is not.
The following possibilities for the role of the L1 will be dealt with:

i. A position which is common to much of the work to be discussed in this
chapter is that UG is available in second language acquisition but cannot
necessarily interact immediately with the L2 input; the learner's initial
hypothesis about the L2 data is that the L1 parameter setting applies to it
(e.g. Hilles 1986; White 1985c, 1986a). The learner uses the L1 parameter
value as a way of organizing the L2 data, resulting in transfer effects in the
interlanguage. However, resetting to the appropriate L2 value is eventually

possible, on the basis of L2 input interacting with UG.

ii. In contrast to this position is one which assumes that UG is effectively dead but is partially accessible via the L1 (Bley-Vroman 1989; Ritchie 1983). On this view, L2 learners should only be able to access aspects of UG which are exemplified in the L1, and this will include L1 parameter settings.

Although both these views assume that the L1 parameter setting will be applied to the L2, there is a crucial difference between them, concerning the issue of whether the L2 learner is capable of resetting a parameter to the appropriate L2 value. On the first view, parameter resetting will be possible, whereas on the second one it will not (or rather, it will only be possible if the L2 value is explicitly obvious from the L2 input without the aid of UG). Thus, any research that demonstrates the operation of the L1 value of a parameter in L2 acquisition is actually neutral between the UG hypothesis and the UG-is-dead hypothesis, but research which demonstrates evidence of resetting to the L2 value favours only the UG hypothesis.

iii. A stronger version of the UG-is-dead hypothesis is also represented in this chapter, namely that the L2 learner's language cannot be described in terms of UG parameters at all, not even the L1 values (Clahsen and Muysken 1986). Other kinds of rule-system are adopted, arrived at via general problem-solving procedures and cognitive strategies.

iv. A final possibility is that UG operates identically in L1 and L2, interacting with the L1 data for L1 acquisition and the L2 data for L2 acquisition. On this view, L1 parameter settings should have no effect: the L2 data should trigger the appropriate L2 value of a parameter. We shall consider this view in more detail in the next two chapters; for the present, it suffices to point out that evidence for the adoption of the L1 setting by an L2 learner is evidence against this position.

Although they differ in their views as to the role of the L1, the first and last positions outlined above share the assumption that ILs are natural languages, constrained by UG. In other words, both views assume that the L2 learner unconsciously imposes organization on the L2 input, creating a mental grammar which accounts for the data, and both views assume that UG severely constrains what that grammar can be like. They agree that a UG parameter value is applied to the L2 input; they differ as to what that value is, that is, as to whether or not the L2 learner uses the L1 parameter value as a preliminary way of interpreting the L2 input. Both these views predict that errors which violate principles of UG will not be found in L2 acquisition.

Many parameters of UG are assumed to be binary, having only two values. If L2 learners are guided by UG, there are only two possibilities for such parameters in the interlanguage grammar, namely that learners adopt either the L1 value or the L2. However, there are other possibilities consistent with the assumption that UG still operates in second language acquisition. Recently, there have been proposals for multi-valued parameters (e.g. Wexler and Manzini 1987). In such cases, L2 learners might adopt a parameter setting which is found neither in the L1 nor in the L2 but which is nevertheless an option available in natural language (Finer and Broselow 1986). In this chapter, we shall concentrate on parameters with binary values; we shall turn to other situations in Chapter 6.

4.3 Methodological issues

Many of the methodological issues discussed in Chapter 3 are also relevant here. L2 learners must have achieved a level which is appropriate to the parameter value being tested. In other words, some kind of implicit or explicit syntax test is desirable, in addition to any tests for parameter settings. The use of native speaker control groups is also highly desirable, in order to establish target language norms, to ensure that native speakers do indeed have the kinds of intuitions about their mother tongue that linguists assume, and to guarantee that any problems that language learners exhibit are not due to quirks of particular sentences.

Furthermore, since a major question is whether L2 learners start off with one setting and switch to another, either longitudinal studies of the same learners or cross-sectional studies of learners at different levels are required, to see if there is evidence of parameter resetting.

Since many parameters link clusters of syntactic properties, one needs to look for evidence of clustering in second language acquisition. Clustering should be expected both in the case where the learner carries over the L1 value of a parameter and where the L2 value is achieved. Learners who transfer the L1 value of the parameter ought to transfer the whole cluster of properties. When learners acquire a parameter setting relevant to L2 , all properties associated with it should be acquired together. The concept of clustering gives a much more sophisticated view of transfer than traditional

Contrastive Analysis which simply says that surface differences will lead to transfer or difficulty, and which does not expect certain effects to be linked to each other.

Ideally, research should look at a particular parameter from both directions, so to speak. That is, suppose that a parameter with two settings, A and B, is being investigated. It is useful to compare learners whose L1 has value A learning an L2 with value B with learners whose L1 has value B learning an L2 with value A. This is because different effects may arise, depending which setting is found in the L1 and which in the L2.

Although the studies to be discussed here are directed at situations where the parameter settings in the L1 and L2 are different, several of them use control groups where the L1 and L2 share the same parameter setting. This is very important; it ensures that any problems of the experimental groups are indeed due to parametric differences between the L1 and L2 and not to problems encountered by all learners regardless of L1.

In investigating principles of UG, researchers have focussed on whether or not L2 learners produce or accept sentences which would constitute violations of UG, or interpret sentences in ways inconsistent with UG, devising methodologies to control the types of sentences under consideration (see Chapter 3). If L2 learners are guided by UG, they should know (unconsciously) that UG violations are ungrammatical; they should not produce them and should reject them in a grammaticality judgment task.

In investigating parameters, it is also necessary to control the sentence types being investigated, to ensure that structures relevant to a parameter are tested for. However, instead of looking at how learners treat UG violations, the question of concern is which parameter setting is reflected in the interlanguage. In many cases, a sentence type that is grammatical in the L1 will be ungrammatical in the L2, and vice versa, and tests must be devised which allow one to assess whether or not the L2 learner knows the relevant properties of the L2.

In certain cases, spontaneous production data can be used more effectively when investigating parameters than they could in the investigation of other principles. If an inappropriate parameter setting is adopted, errors are predicted that reflect the operation of the 'wrong' parameter setting. Such errors do not indicate that the L2 learner is violating UG but, rather, the choice of a possible parameter value permitted by UG, though not the correct one for the target language.

4.4   Some parameters of UG

In current linguistic theory, a number of different parameters have been proposed, some of which have been investigated in the L2 acquisition context. These will be discussed in this chapter and in Chapter 6. Most parameters relate to the various levels and principles presented in Chapter 1, and are proposed to account for differences in the ways principles operate from language to language. An exception is the Prodrop Parameter (4.5), which does not fit in any obvious way into the levels and principles discussed earlier.

In 4.6, a parameter which relates to X bar theory, namely the parameter of Head-position, will be considered; it has two values, head-initial and head-final (see also 1.9). In 4.7.1, the Empty Category Principle will be discussed. Parametric variation here concerns what can count as a proper governor (1.8.2.8). In 4.7.2, we shall look at Subjacency again, the principle which places limitations on syntactic movement (1.8.2.4). Bounding nodes for Subjacency are parameterized, in that languages vary as to the kinds of syntactic categories that material can be extracted from.

In Chapter 6, we turn to a parameter that relates to Case Theory (1.8.2.5), namely the Adjacency Condition on Case Assignment, as well as parameters relating to the Binding Theory (.1.8.2.7), particularly to the choice of governing categories for anaphors and pronouns.

These parameters by no means exhaust the possibilities currently being investigated within linguistic theory. They have been chosen because they are considered by researchers to offer interesting predictions for L2 acquisition and to be amenable to psycholinguistic investigation.

4.5   The Prodrop Parameter

One of the first parameters to be proposed in linguistic theory was the Prodrop or Null Subject Parameter (Chomsky 1981a; Jaeggli 1982; Rizzi 1982). There are several different proposals as to what precisely constitutes the Prodrop Parameter, i.e., what properties cluster with it, and how this clustering is to be accounted for; these differences are reflected in the L2 acquisition literature. All proposals agree on the following: there are certain languages, such as Italian and Spanish, which allow subject pronouns to be omitted; this is the *prodrop* or *null subject* phenomenon. These languages exhibit the [+ prodrop] value of the parameter. Other languages, such as English, always require lexical subjects,[1] representing the [− prodrop] value. In other words, the subject position in an English sentence cannot be empty, whereas it may in Spanish, as shown in (1):

(1)   *Anda   muy   ocupada*
       Is   very busy
       'She is very busy'

[+ prodrop] languages also allow lexical pronouns to appear in subject position, with certain discourse constraints on their use. However, where English would require a pleonastic pronoun (*it* or *there*), null subjects are always required in [+ prodrop] languages.

Although accounts of the Prodrop Parameter differ considerably in detail, they try to formalize the observation that [+ prodrop] is usually associated with languages with rich inflectional systems, so that the nature of the missing subject can easily be recovered.[2] In (1), feminine agreement on the verb and the adjective indicates that the missing subject is *she*.

In addition, other properties cluster with the presence or absence of null subjects, although there is disagreement as to what all these properties are. Two versions of the Prodrop Parameter and its cluster of properties are presented in Table 4.1, in simplified form. These versions have been adopted in L2 acquisition research on this parameter. The only difference between them that is of concern here is that version 1 assumes that subject-verb inversion and *that*-trace sequences[3] are part of the cluster of properties belonging to the [+ prodrop] value of the parameter, while version 2 assumes that they are not.

There is considerable discussion in the literature as to whether one of the values of the Prodrop Parameter can be considered unmarked and the other marked, and if so, which is which. Markedness will be explored in Chapters 5 and 6, and we will look at the Prodrop Parameter from a markedness perspective there. Here, we shall simply treat the parameter as having two different values, [+ prodrop] and [− prodrop], without considering their markedness values.

Most of the prodrop research conducted so far looks only at the acquisition of English by native speakers of Spanish, that is, a [+ prodrop] L1 and a [− prodrop] L2.[4] Phinney (1987) looks at the parameter from both perspectives, including a group of English learners of Spanish, i.e., a [− prodrop] L1 and a [+ prodrop] L2. This raises the issue that the same kinds

Table 4.1   The Prodrop Parameter

	[+ prodrop] (e.g. Spanish, Italian)	*[− prodrop]* (e.g. English)

Version 1 assumed by
Chomsky 1981,
Liceras 1988b,
Phinney 1987,
Rizzi 1982
White 1985, 1986
	Null subjects
	No pleonastic pronouns
	Rich verbal agreement
	Subject-verb inversion in
	  declaratives, e.g.
	   Vino Juan
	   Came John
	   'John came'
	That-trace sequences,
	e.g.
	   Quien dijiste que vino?
	   Who said that came
	   'Who did you say came?'
		Lexical subjects
		Pleonastic pronouns
		Lack of rich agreement
		No subject-verb inversion in
		  declaratives, e.g.
		   *Came John
		
		No *that*-trace sequences,
		e.g.
		   *Who did you say that came?

Version 2 assumed by
Hilles 1986, Hyams 1986
	Null subjects
	No pleonastic pronouns
	Auxiliaries and main verbs
	  form one category
		Lexical subjects
		Pleonastic pronouns
		Auxiliaries are distinct from
		  main verbs

of data may be less revealing in one of the two contexts. Let us consider what could count as evidence for the retention of the L1 value of the parameter. If the L1 value is applied to the L2, the inappropriate value of the parameter is predicted to be realized in the interlanguage grammar. Thus, when the L1 is Spanish and the L2 is English, sentences with missing subjects are expected in production data, and if they occur, this is support for transfer of the L1 value.

On the other hand, when the L1 is English and the L2 Spanish, production data cannot give a totally clear indication of the adoption of the inappropriate parameter value. The problem is that [+ prodrop] languages do not absolutely require null subjects (except in the case of impersonal constructions); they allow pronominal subjects as well. Therefore, if native speakers of [− prodrop] languages tend to use pronouns in their production, this is not a guarantee that they have failed to reset the parameter. They may not yet have worked out the precise discourse considerations that govern use of null versus lexical pronouns. In other words, there are two different things that an L2 learner of a [+ prodrop] language has to acquire:

(i) the fact that null subjects are permitted, and (ii) the circumstances in which the language actually makes use of the fact that null subjects are permitted.[5] Failure to acquire the second says nothing about the acquisition of the first. A learner could successfully reset the parameter and yet still not have total command of the discourse constraints governing the use of lexical pronouns, leading to overuse or underuse of null subjects. While accurate use of null subjects suggests that learners have indeed reset the parameter to the L2 value, data from sources other than spontaneous production may be required to establish whether L2 learners of Spanish who use lexical pronouns have really failed to reset the parameter.

4.5.1 *White*

White (1985c, 1986a) investigates whether Spanish learners of English transfer the L1 value of the Prodrop Parameter to the L2 in two related studies, (using different subjects in each). Subjects were adult learners of ESL. In the White (1986a) study, the experimental group consisted of native speakers of [+ prodrop] languages, 32 Spanish and 2 Italian. A control group consisted of 37 native speakers of French, a [− prodrop] language. Subjects were in three intermediate levels of the Continuing Education Programme at McGill University in Montreal, Canada. French and Spanish subjects at each level were equated for proficiency, according to McGill's placement tests.

There were two tasks: the first was a grammaticality judgment task and the second was a written question formation task. The grammaticality judgment task had twenty-eight sentences, sixteen of which were ungrammatical sentences exemplifying three of the properties clustering with the [+ prodrop] setting (version 1), namely null subjects, subject-verb inversion and *that*-trace sequences. In other words, they were ungrammatical in English but would have been grammatical in Spanish. The other sentences were grammatical equivalents of these. Subjects had to respond *correct, incorrect*, or *not sure* to the sentences, and to try to correct the sentences they thought incorrect. Such corrections allow the experimenter to establish whether subjects are rejecting sentences for appropriate reasons.

Results are summarized in Table 4.2. They are reported here in terms of accuracy, that is correctly identifying ungrammatical (U) sentences as ungrammatical and grammatical (G) sentences as grammatical. Both the Spanish/Italian group and the French group are accurate on all three types

Table 4.2 Accuracy responses in the grammaticality judgment task, in percentages (White 1986a)

Sentence type	Spanish	French
Subjectless (U)	61	89
With subjects (G)	90	97
VS order (U)	91	96
SV order (G)	81	85
that-trace (U)	23	35
Other extractions (G)	79	79

of grammatical sentences. There are significant differences between the French and Spanish speakers in terms of their accuracy on subjectless sentences: the Spanish are much more likely to accept these than the French, suggesting that the L1 value of the Prodrop Parameter has been carried over, for this property at least. When results are broken down by level, there is evidence of improved accuracy with increasing level, suggesting that Spanish learners are able to reset this parameter.

However, differences do not show up on the other two supposed properties of the parameter: both groups accurately reject VS order and both groups performed very poorly on *that*-trace sequences, failing to reject them. Liceras (1988b), Zobl (p.c.) point out that the sentences chosen to exemplify VS order might have been inappropriate in two different ways:

(a) according to Liceras, VS order in Spanish sounds better with so-called ergative verbs (Burzio 1981) but the verbs used in White's studies were not of this class, and (b) this order is subject to discourse considerations in Spanish that were not covered in this task. These are methodological problems which could be corrected by more careful choice of test sentences.

As far as the *that*-trace results are concerned, again there is a methodological problem with the choice of sentences. The *that*-trace sentences may well have been too difficult for the subjects; apparent accuracy on the corresponding grammatical sentences could simply have been due to a strategy of responding *correct*. Further problems may have been introduced by the fact that sentences were not controlled for vocabulary choice or length and by the fact that there were fewer sentences relevant to the *that*-trace aspect of the parameter.

The possibility that difficulties with complex sentences were causing the low accuracy on *that*-trace violations was controlled for in the question formation task. This task was designed to find out whether language learners would produce *that*-trace sequences when questioning embedded subjects. Subjects were given 12 declarative sentences, each of which contained an underlined phrase, and they were asked to question that phrase. For example, the sentence in (2a) could receive a response like (2b):

(2) a. Elizabeth believes that *her sister* will be late
     b. Who does Elizabeth believe will be late?

There were three test sentences where the underlined phrase was the subject of the embedded clause (as in (2a)). Nine other sentences required the formation of simple questions, and also questions on material in the embedded clause other than the subject. These served as a syntax test; results were discounted if subjects could not correctly form questions for these sentences.

After removing subjects who could not in general form questions correctly, the results show a clear difference between the Spanish and the French subjects. As can be seen in Table 4.3, both groups made errors in questioning the subject of an embedded clause, but the Spanish were significantly more likely than the French to produce a *that*-trace sequence in the process, suggesting the operation of the L1 parameter setting.

Table 4.3 Results from the question formation task, in percentages (White 1986a)

	Correct	That-trace	Other errors
Spanish (n=22)	17	71	12
French (n=30)	20	42	38

The results from these two tasks suggest that the Prodrop Parameter is transferred from L1 to L2, but only partially so, since the VS sentences were correctly rejected by Spanish learners as well as by the French. What can we conclude from the apparent failure of prodrop characteristics to cluster in the interlanguage grammar? One possibility, of course, is that parameters of UG are no longer accessible to L2 learners. However, there are also several alternative explanations. Some relate to the test methodology; it has already been mentioned above that the sentences chosen to exemplify VS order may have been inappropriate. Other researchers have found VS sentences in production data (Rutherford 1989; Schumann 1978), particularly when ergative verbs are used. With a more rigorous choice of test sentences, judgment data and production data might coincide, suggesting that this aspect of the parameter is transferred as well as the possibility of null subjects.

Another possibility relates to issues within linguistic theory. As shown in Table 4.1, there is some disagreement as to which properties cluster with the Prodrop Parameter. While verb-subject orders are possible in [+ prodrop] languages, they might not be a consequence of the parameter but independent from it (as assumed in version 2). In that case, one would not expect L2 learners to behave similarly with respect to treatment of subject-less sentences and VS order.

4.5.2 *Phinney*

Phinney (1987) also assumes version 1 of the Prodrop Parameter. She looks at two properties: the presence versus absence of subject pronouns, and the agreement system. Her study is useful in that it is the only one to look at the operation of the parameter in both directions i.e. L1 Spanish to L2 English (ESL groups) and L1 English to L2 Spanish (SSL groups). Unfortunately, her subjects are not truly matched. She has two ESL groups, students at the University of Puerto Rico, who had received twelve years of English instruction at school; in spite of this, they were assessed as high beginners or low intermediate at the university. Two SSL groups were students at the University of Massachusetts at Amherst, USA, and had not necessarily had any exposure to Spanish before attending the university; thus, in contrast to the ESL groups, many of them were genuinely adult learners. They were also classed as beginners and low intermediate. Since these assessments come from two very different universities, and concern two different languages, it is not clear whether beginners and low intermediate are really equivalent in the two language groups. Ideally, for this kind of research, one needs appropriate versions of the same measure of proficiency to be applied to all subjects. Not surprisingly, measures for circumstances like these are hard to come by.[6]

Phinney uses evidence from written production data, namely free compositions. Again, it is not clear that the task was identical in the two situations, since she does not report whether all groups were given the same topic to write about, and the conditions were certainly different (an exam in one case and a class assignment in the other). These compositions were examined for verbal agreement, and for omission of subject pronouns (ESL groups) and overuse of pronouns (SSL groups).

Table 4.4   *Percentage of omission of pronoun subjects by ESL and SSL groups (Phinney 1987)*

	ESL1	ESL2	SSL1	SSL2
Referential	13	6	83	65
Pleonastic	56	76	100	100

Verbal agreement was quite accurate in all groups. Use of null subjects is summarized in Table 4.4. This is incorrect for English, and correct for Spanish. While referential pronoun omission by the ESL groups was low, they appeared to be following Spanish discourse rules, omitting referential pronouns in subordinate or conjoined clauses, where reference was obvious from context, but not in sentence initial position. Pleonastic pronouns, on the other hand, were much more likely to be omitted by the ESL groups; these are constructions where pronouns are absolutely prohibited in Spanish but required in English. These results are consistent with the hypothesis that the native speakers of Spanish are carrying over the L1 value of the parameter (recall that this value allows both null and lexical pronouns).

The native speakers of English, on the other hand, correctly omitted both referential and pleonastic pronoun subjects in Spanish, and never tried to use a lexical pronoun as subject of impersonal constructions, suggesting that they had reset the parameter to the L2 value.

Why are the results from the two language groups different, as far as evidence for parameter resetting is concerned? One possibility has already been raised; the learners are not strictly comparable. The SSL groups might in fact be more advanced than the ESL groups, so that the same stages of second language development are not being tapped here. A theoretically more interesting possibility is that crucial differences are to be expected, depending on which language is the L1 and which the L2. This relates to the issue of whether parameter settings have unmarked and marked values, which will be discussed in Chapters 5 and 6.

4.5.3   *Hilles*

Like White and Phinney, Hilles (1986) assumes that learners whose mother tongue is [+ prodrop] will start out by applying this value of the parameter to the L2, and that they will eventually reset to [− prodrop]. She makes use of longitudinal production data from one subject, a 12-year old Spanish-speaking boy, whose acquisition of English was followed over a period of 10 months.

Hilles adopts version 2 of the Prodrop Parameter, which assumes that null subjects are incompatible with a distinct category of auxiliary verbs (Hyams 1986). In early weeks, the learner omitted subject referential pronouns extensively (on 80% of possible occasions for use of a pronoun), suggesting that the L1 value had been transferred. Pronoun omission declined over the period of investigation, consistent with resetting to the L2 value. Hilles found a relationship between the emergence of auxiliary verbs as a distinct category (as required by English) and the decline in use of null subjects, suggesting that when the parameter is reset from the L1 to L2 value, this affects the cluster of properties associated with the parameter.

Hilles also assumes, following Hyams (1986), that resetting from the [+ prodrop] to the [− prodrop] value will be triggered when the learner notices the pleonastic pronouns *it* and *there* in English. Hyams claims that these indicate the need for grammatical subjects in languages like English; they cannot be there for any other reason, since they have no meaning or pragmatic force. Hilles offers evidence that the change from the [+ prodrop] setting to the [− prodrop] setting occurs at about the time when pleonastic pronouns are first used by this learner, suggesting that they may have served as the trigger for resetting. However, as discussed above, Phinney's results suggest that pleonastic pronouns are actually the last to be acquired, indicating that they may be a consequence rather than a cause of parameter resetting, and that something else must serve as a trigger for resetting from one value of the parameter to another in second language acquisition.

4.5.4   *The Prodrop Parameter: summary of findings*

To summarize the findings on the Prodrop Parameter, all three studies show some evidence for transfer of the L1 parameter setting, and in some cases for resetting to the L2 value, and this evidence comes both from grammaticality judgment tasks and from spoken and written production data, and from subjects who learn as adults as well as child learners. As far as clustering is concerned, only some of the properties associated with the parameter cluster with it in second language acquisition. The clearest evidence of transfer comes from the acceptance and use of null subjects by native speakers of Spanish. This alone would not be particularly compelling evidence for parameters of UG in second language acquisition, since it would also be predicted on a traditional Contrastive Analysis theory. However, Contrastive Analysis would not predict the difference in the two situations that Phinney looked at (i.e., for resetting from the [− prodrop] to the [+ prodrop] value but not from the [+ prodrop] to the [− prodrop] value).

4.6 Word order parameters

In this section, we shall look at research which focuses on phrase structure and word order. Once again, a binary parameter of UG will be considered. The parameter of Head-position (1.9) has the settings *head-initial*, where the ordering is head before complement (i.e., nouns, verbs and prepositions occur before their complements), and *head-final*, where the ordering is complement before head (i.e., nouns, verbs and prepositions occur after their complements). Head-position usually holds consistently across syntactic categories within a language. Head-initial languages are sometimes referred to as *right-branching* and head-final as *left-branching*. Much of the work that has been done on this area in L2 acquisition assumes an earlier formulation, in terms of a parameter of principal branching direction (PBD), which is also concerned with properties of phrase structure and word order, but which covers a wider range of structures, including ones where a head-complement relationship is not involved, such as adverbial clauses.

One might think that parameter resetting for a learner whose L1 and L2 differ with respect to head-position or branching direction ought not to be particularly problematic or interesting. After all, differences between a head-initial and a head-final language are fairly basic, show up in a variety of simple structures, and ought to be obvious to a language learner, even in early stages.

However, Flynn (1984, 1987b) argues that other properties of language cluster with head-position, properties relating to interpretation of pronouns, making the case where the L1 and the L2 head-positions differ more complicated than suggested above. She argues that the parameter of Head-position, or Principal Branching Direction, is operative in second language acquisition, and that where the parameter setting differs in L1 and L2 there will be effects on the L2 learner. Her position is a mixture of claims (i) and (iv) outlined in 4.2, in that she assumes L1 and L2 acquisition to be basically alike, with UG guiding both, but also that there is an effect of L1 parameter settings, an effect of delay and difficulty in acquiring the L2 setting, rather than transfer of the L1 setting.

Another case where the Head-position Parameter does not operate in a straight-forward fashion arises in German, where the position of the head is not consistent across all categories, and the position of the verb varies, depending on the clause type (see 4.6.2.1 for details). Clahsen and Muysken (1986) claim that UG no longer operates in adult L2 acquisition (position (iii) in 4.2), and that adult learners of German have great difficulty in acquiring the intricacies of German word order, dealing with it in ways that are consistent with neither the L1 nor the L2 value for UG parameters.

4.6.1 *Flynn*

Flynn's work (e.g. 1984, 1987a, 1987b, 1987c) was originally undertaken assuming a parameter of Principal Branching Direction (PBD) proposed by Lust (1981, 1983, 1986) to account for certain aspects of L1 acquisition:

> PBD refers to the branching direction which holds consistently in unmarked form over major recursive structures of a language, where "major recursive structures" are defined to include relative clause formation of complex NP, adverbial subordinate clause, and sentential complementation. (Lust 1983, p.138)

In addition, the following Directionality Constraint on L1 acquisition is assumed:

> In early child language, the direction of grammatical anaphora accords with the Principal Branching Direction (PBD) of the specific language being acquired.......Specifically, in RB (right-branching) languages, early anaphora is constrained in a forward direction; in LB (left-branching), it is constrained in a backward direction. (Lust 1983, pp.141-2)

Anaphora is involved when an NP and a pronoun are coreferential. For example, in (3a) and (3b), the pronoun *he* can be coreferential with the nounphrase *John*, usually referred to as the *antecedent*:

(3) a. After *John* had eaten, *he* went to a movie
     b. After *he* had eaten, *John* went to a movie

Lust's claim, then, is that in right-branching (RB) languages like English, children will strongly prefer sentences like (3a) where the antecedent precedes the anaphor, a case of *forwards anaphora* (FA), and avoid cases like (3b), which are known as *backwards anaphora* (BA).

This Directionality Constraint is an attempt to account for the fact that children learning English as their L1 avoid backwards anaphora. In elicited imitation tasks, young English-speaking children are significantly more successful at imitating sentences with forwards anaphora than backwards anaphora, and often convert backwards anaphora sentences like (3b) to forwards anaphora sentences like (3a). In act-out tasks, children will interpret *he* and *John* coreferentially in sentences like (3a) but will choose an antecedent outside the sentence in cases like (3b) (Lust 1983; Solan 1983).

However, it is quite possible that these experimental results do not really reflect children's grammatical competence but simply their preferences. English allows both forwards and backwards anaphora; it may be that children know this, but choose not to make use of backwards anaphora, for pragmatic reasons (cf. Reinhart 1986). Recently, a number of researchers have shown that English children do allow backwards anaphora in their grammars, given suitable contexts (Crain and McKee 1986; Goodluck 1987; Lasnik and Crain 1985). O'Grady et al. (1986) have shown that L1 acquirers of left-branching languages like Japanese also prefer forwards anaphora, contrary to Lust's predictions. Such results call the Directionality Constraint into question.

In any case, there is an important difference in the status of the PBD Parameter and the Directionality Constraint. PBD is a parameter of UG. Although this parameter has been superseded by others, the general idea that there are parameters which account for word order is fairly uncontroversial. The Directionality Constraint, linking PBD and anaphora, on the other hand, is much more questionable. Most languages violate this constraint, allowing backwards anaphora, so it **cannot** be a constraint of UG.

Like Lust, Flynn (1984, 1987c) assumes (a) that there is a parameter of PBD, and (b) that there is a Directionality Constraint which relates anaphora acquisition to branching direction. She looks at whether the second language acquisition of anaphora is constrained by branching direction; recently, she has recast her claims in terms of Head-position (e.g. 1987a, 1987b).

Flynn's subjects are adult learners of ESL, 51 native speakers of Spanish, and 53 native speakers of Japanese, divided into three proficiency levels, low, intermediate and high. English, the L2, is a head-initial, or right-branching, language. Spanish is head-initial like English, whereas Japanese is head-final, or left-branching. If L2 learners are sensitive to the branching direction of English and guided by a Directionality Constraint, they should find forwards anaphora easier in English than backwards.

Flynn's precise claim as to the role of the L1 parameter setting is not entirely clear. She argues that Spanish subjects will show the forward directionality preference for anaphora because Spanish and English have the same branching direction. On the other hand, she does not want to claim that the Japanese will transfer the PBD (or head-position) of Japanese or their purported preference for backwards anaphora:[7]

> Patterns of acquisition should be similar to L1 acquisition .... both where the head direction[8] of the L1 matches the L2 (L1HD=L2HD) and where it does not (L1HD≠L2HD)..... When L1HD≠L2HD, L2 learners must assign a new value to the parameter, and we would expect acquisition patterns to correspond to early L1 acquisition patterns for this parameter..... When L1HD=L2HD, ... acquisition patterns should correspond to later stages in the L1 acquisition of these structures (1987b, p.84).

In other words, there will be differences in the L2 acquisition of English anaphora, depending on the L1 of the learner. These will not be reflected in the form of the adoption of the L1 parameter setting; rather, the Japanese will have to start from scratch, and so will behave like very young children learning their L1s, whereas the Spanish will be able to bypass this stage because their L1 shares the same BD as the L2.

If one takes this passage literally, Flynn would have to predict that Japanese learners of ESL will show a **greater** preference for forwards anaphora than Spanish learners, since early L1 learners of English are the ones who show the strong preference for forwards anaphora. In fact, her claim is just the opposite of this: she expects the Spanish to show a forward directionality preference, not the Japanese.

Flynn's subjects were tested with an imitation task and an act-out comprehension task, both using adverbial clauses. The sentence types used in the imitation tests are exemplified in (4), where the pronouns can be interpreted with either NP in the main clause, or with someone outside of the sentence. When the adverbial clause is in initial position (as in 4a), there is backwards anaphora (BA) if the antecedent is one of the other NPs in the sentence.

(4) a. When he entered the office, the janitor questioned the man (LB/BA)
     b. The mayor questioned the president when he entered the room (RB/FA)
     c. When the professor opened the package, he answered the man (LB/FA)

Flynn's assumption is that the post-posed (RB) position for the adverbial clause is more basic in English and Spanish. Her claim, then, is that Spanish learners will have the greatest advantage with sentences like (4b), where the sentence is right-branching and anaphora direction is forwards. (However, it is not clear in what sense a main clause counts as a head with an adverbial clause as its complement.)

Unlike many of the experiments previously described, Flynn is very careful to pretest for vocabulary and to control for sentence length, and to get independent measures of her subjects' ESL proficiency.[9] Unfortunately, there are factors that prevent the subjects' true competence with respect to anaphora from revealing itself in an imitation task. Sentences like (4a) and (4b) are three-ways ambiguous and one of the possible interpretations involves an antecedent not mentioned in the sentence. If subjects correctly imitate these sentences, we simply cannot tell what their interpretation of the relationship between pronoun and NP is; in particular, we cannot tell whether a sentence internal or external referent for the pronoun is being assumed. But in order to show that L2 learners are behaving like L1 learners at various stages, we **must** be able to tell what interpretation they assign to the pronouns in the test sentences. The backwards/forwards anaphora issue only relates to choices of antecedents within a sentence, not within the discourse in general.

Such problems do not arise with the other task that Flynn uses, namely an act-out comprehension task, where subjects were required to manipulate shapes in response to test sentences like the following:

(5) a. When it turned over, the blue circle touched the red triangle (LB/BA)
     b. The yellow square touched the red triangle, when it turned around (RB/FA)

Here, subjects' responses will more clearly indicate how they interpret pronouns, since one can tell what they consider the antecedent of *it* to be by the object they manipulate.

In general, Flynn's results from all tasks show that Spanish subjects at all levels were more successful in imitating and acting-out English complex sentences than the Japanese, including sentences with both types of anaphora, with the position of the adverbial clause varied, and ones without any anaphora. This might, as Flynn suggests, reflect the fact that Japanese BD is different from English, whereas Spanish is the same; it might also be due to other typological differences between the two languages. Alternatively, it might just mean that the ESL placement tests were in fact not capturing proficiency differences between the Spanish and Japanese subjects, so that the groups were not strictly comparable (Bley-Vroman and Chaudron 1988).

The results specific to anaphora do not fit clearly into Flynn's hypotheses. In the imitation test, the Spanish subjects at the **mid level only** were significantly more accurate on forwards anaphora than backward; the Japanese showed no significant difference between forward and backward anaphora and neither did the low and high level Spanish. Thus, if anyone was behaving like L1 acquirers of English in finding forwards anaphora easier to imitate accurately, it was only one of the Spanish groups. The low and high Spanish and all the Japanese groups behaved alike in **not** showing a preference for forwards anaphora.

The results from the act-out task appear to contradict those from the imitation task. As before, the Spanish were generally better at the task but this time the Japanese were significantly more accurate on the forwards anaphora sentences than the backwards ones, while the Spanish showed no significant difference between the two anaphora types.

While Flynn's results demonstrate that her Spanish subjects had fewer difficulties than her Japanese subjects with English adverbial clause structures, it is not clear that this has anything to do with similarities and differences between the head-position or branching directions of the languages concerned. As far as the Directionality Constraint is concerned, the preference for forwards anaphora shows up in one of the Spanish groups for the imitation tasks, and in the Japanese groups for the act-out task. What is more striking is that most groups on most tasks do not show a difference between forwards and backwards anaphora. In a replication of Flynn's imitation tasks with Arabic learners of English, Eubank (1989) also found no significant difference between responses to the sentences involving BA and FA.

Do these results mean that attempts to account for L2 acquisition in terms of parameters of UG should be abandoned? It is important to recognize that the somewhat equivocal nature of Flynn's results does not mean that we can assume the non-operation of UG in second language acquisition, nor does it mean that a parameter-setting model is incorrect; it simply means that inappropriate parameters and constraints have been identified for this particular aspect of the grammar. The general questions which Flynn addresses remain valid, even if researchers have to revise their notions of the parameters in question. Recent criticisms of Flynn (Bley-Vroman and Chaudron 1988) have only shown that a particular version of a parameter setting model is not supported, not that the model is incorrect in principle. Flynn's insight that parameter theory has the potential to account both for L1 influence and for universal aspects of L2 acquisition is an important one, and one that we should continue to develop.

Flynn has identified two very important issues for second language acquisition research, namely the role of word order parameters, and the question of anaphora interpretation. Her problems stem from trying to combine these, and from considering the issues only in terms of a very limited range of sentence types. I agree with Flynn that there is a parameter of Head-position and that this would have to be assigned a new value for the L2 where L1≠L2. However, positive evidence for this difference will show up in very simple sentences, so L2 learners should already have reset this parameter by the time they have to deal with anaphora in complex sentences with adverbial clauses.

Anaphora in L2 acquisition should now be investigated independently of word order parameters.[10] Languages show anaphora prohibitions and possibilities that are simply not captured by Lust's Directionality Constraint. The crucial concept in accounting for these is c-command (1.8.2.6), not branching direction. (See Reinhart (1986) for further discussion.) According to current linguistic theory, anaphora interpretation falls out from the Binding Theory (1.8.2.7). Thus, in order to see whether UG still operates in second language acquisition in the domain of anaphora, we need experiments that look at Binding Theory itself: do L2 learners observe it or do they not? Do they observe it in simple sentences as well as complex? If parameters are involved, what are they and what are their effects? How do L2 learners treat reciprocals and reflexives? (Some of these questions are addressed by research discussed in Chapter 6.)

In fact, Flynn's results appear to be perfectly consistent with the operation of the Binding Theory in L2 acquisition. Pronouns must be free in their governing categories and referential NPs must be entirely free in the sentence (1.8.2.7). If these conditions are met, as they are in Flynn's test sentences, coreference is possible (but not necessary) between a pronoun and some other NP in the sentence. Hence, both backwards and forwards anaphora are allowed and there is no predicted difference between the two sentence types. However, the Binding Theory is not incompatible with additional pragmatic or processing constraints favouring forwards anaphora, such as those proposed by Reinhart (1986), or Bley-Vroman and Chaudron (1988), which can account for those occasions when Flynn's subjects did show a forwards anaphora preference.

One of the two issues investigated by Flynn, namely word order, is also considered by Clahsen and Muysken (1986), Clahsen (1988). Unlike Flynn, who assumes that word order parameters are still available to L2 learners, Clahsen and Muysken argue that they are not, and that L2 learners do not even make use of the L1 parameter setting as a means of dealing with the L2.

4.6.2 Clahsen and Muysken

So far in this chapter we have looked at the question of the potential effects of the L1 parameter setting on the way the learner deals with the L2. It might be objected that allowing properties of the L1 grammar to count as evidence for the operation of UG leaves one with no way of disproving that UG operates in second language acquisition. If the UG hypothesis is not in principle falsifiable, it loses much of its interest. In this section, we will look at the work of Clahsen and Muysken (1986), who assume that UG operates in L1 acquisition but not in adult L2 acquisition.[11] Instead, they argue, adults hypothesize rules on the basis of general learning strategies and processing constraints, and the rules that adult learners come up with are 'unnatural', i.e., do not observe the constraints that UG places on natural languages. As Clahsen and Muysken's arguments concern properties of German word order, especially the question of whether learners of German treat the verb phrase as head-initial or head-final, it is appropriate to consider them here, in the context of the parameter of Head-position.

4.6.2.1 *Properties of German word order*
In order to understand the acquisition problem that German raises, some facts about German word order must be presented. At the level of S-struc-

ture, German is verb-final in subordinate clauses but not in main clauses. For the syntactic categories NP and PP, German is head-initial at all levels, and in all clause types. Most generative linguists assume that the subordinate clause order represents the D-structure order for German. In other words, the German VP is head-final, but other categories, such as NP and PP, are head-initial.

In German main clauses, the finite verb is found in second position (V2), after the subject (S) or a topicalized element, such as the direct object (O) or an adverbial (A), as in (6):

(6)   a.   *Die Kinder   essen   das Brot*   (SVO)
            The children eat   the bread
       b.   *Das Brot   essen   die Kinder*   (OVS)
            The bread eat   the children
            'The children eat the bread'
       c.   *Nun   essen   die Kinder   das Brot*   (AVSO)
            Now eat   the children the bread
            'Now the children eat the bread'

Where there is both a finite (V^{+F}) and a non-finite verb (V^{-F}) or particle, these are separate in main clauses, with the finite verb in second position and the non-finite verb at the end, as in (7):

(7)   *Die Kinder   haben das Brot   gegessen*   ($S\ V^{+F}\ O\ V^{-F}$)
       the children have the bread eaten
       'The children have eaten the bread'

In embedded clauses, on the other hand, the finite verb is found at the end of the clause, as in (8):

(8)   a.   *Ich glaube dass die Kinder   das Brot   essen*   ($...SOV^{+F}$)
            I believe that the children the bread eat
       b.   *Ich glaube dass die Kinder   das Brot   gegessen*
            I believe that the children the bread eaten
            haben   ($...SOV^{-F}\ V^{+F}$)
            have
            'I believe that the children are eating/have eaten the bread'

On the assumption that German is verb-final, with the underlying word order of SOV, the other orders are accounted for by a rule that moves the finite verb leftwards (e.g. Thiersch 1978). In this tradition, Clahsen and Muysken assume two obligatory movement rules in main clauses. One rule moves the inflected verb to the COMP position, and the other moves some other element (subject, object, adverbial, etc) into a topic position preceding the inflected verb. The finite verb cannot be moved into second position in embedded clauses because the complementizer fills the COMP position to which the inflected verb would normally move.

4.6.2.2 *Acquisition orders in L1 and L2 German*

Clahsen and Muysken review a number of empirical studies of stages of development of verb placement in German L1 and L2 acquisition, and argue that there are crucial differences between the two. Children learning German as their mother tongue predominantly use SOV word order in early stages, even though this is actually ungrammatical in main clauses in German. They suggest that various principles of UG give children access to the underlying order of German. Second language learners with Romance mother tongues, on the other hand, use SVO order, both where this is correct for German, and where it is not. Clahsen and Muysken argue that this is not simply a reflection of the L1 head-initial parameter setting being applied to the L2, since Turkish learners of German also show SVO order, and Turkish is a head-final language. If Turks were accessing the L1 parameter setting, they ought to adopt SOV order.

Clahsen and Muysken make two claims that are relevant to the concerns of this chapter. Both claims assume that UG is inaccessible to L2 learners:

i. L2 learners of German adopt SVO order because they are following a canonical word order strategy (see below), not because they are adopting their L1 parameter setting.

ii. L2 learners of German are incapable of resetting this order to the underlying SOV order that German requires. Since they do, however, eventually produce sentences with the nonfinite verb correctly at the end of main clauses, and with the finite verb at the end of subordinate clauses, Clahsen and Muysken argue that these superficially correct forms are the result of applying various 'unnatural' rules to their SVO order.

The data that Clahsen and Muysken present in support of their arguments are naturalistic production data only, and they do not provide a quantitative analysis of their findings. The surface word orders reflected in the data, and their proposed analyses for each stage, are summarized below in Table 4.5. Discussion here will be confined to the stages relevant to word order within the main clause.

Table 4.5 *Stages of German main clause word order acquisition*

Stage	German L1 acquisition	German L2 acquisition
1	Word orders: S V$^{\pm F}$ O and S O V$^{\pm F}$ Analysis: Underlying SOV order, + optional verb movement rule (not specified for finiteness)	Word order: S V$^{\pm F}$ O Analysis: Underlying SVO order
2	Word orders: S V^{+F} O and S O V$^{\pm F}$ Analysis: SOV, + optional verb movement rule specified for finiteness	Word order: A S V O Analysis: SVO and adverb fronting rule
3	Word orders: S V^{+F} O V^{-F} and A V^{+F} S .... Analysis: SOV + obligatory verb second and topicalization	Word orders: S V^{+F} O V^{-F} and A S V^{+F} O V^{-F} Analysis: SVO, + adverb fronting +movement of non finite elements to the end
4	(L1 acquisition of main clause order completed)	Word order: A V^{+F} S .... Analysis: SVO order, + adverb fronting, + subject-verb inversion

S=Subject, V=verb, O=object, A=adverbial, +F=finite, −F=non finite

Let us first consider the difference between the predominantly SOV word order of the L1 learner and the SVO order of the L2 learner in the first two stages. Clahsen and Muysken (also Clahsen 1984, 1988) attribute the SVO order to a processing strategy, which is not a principle of UG. In particular, learners are assumed to be able to reconstruct the canonical sentence schema of the target language, these schemas being derived from the 'neutral' sentence type, i.e., simple active affirmative sentences (Slobin and Bever 1982). On this definition, the canonical word order of German is SVO. The canonical order strategy assumes that the learner can easily work out what the canonical order is, on the basis of input. This assumption is particularly problematic in the case of German.[12]

In appealing to the canonical order strategy, and in using only production data, Clahsen and Muysken have failed to distinguish between L2 *performance* and the acquisition of L2 *competence*. The strategy does seem to describe the production of the L2 learner (**if** SVO is the canonical order of German). However, it cannot explain the acquisition of that word order on the basis of German input. If you are trying to produce a sentence, it makes sense to stick to some basic order that you have arrived at. The question is: how does one arrive at that order? How is it acquired? The canonical order strategy presupposes what it is supposed to explain. Assume a learner who is just beginning to learn German and who must acquire a word order (right or wrong) to be going along with in the L2. The trouble is that the learner does not have control over the input. If the **speaker** uses sentences which are not in 'canonical' form, it is not clear how the hearer/learner is to avoid these or to detect what the canonical order is. German is a particularly problematic case, allowing a number of surface word orders in declaratives, including: S V O, S $V^{+F}O$ V^{-F}, A V S O, and A V^{+F} S O V^{-F}, in main clauses, and S O V and S O V^{-F} V^{+F} in subordinate clauses. It is simply begging the question to claim that SVO is the canonical order for German and that there is a processing principle which detects this (White 1989b).

Principles of UG are intended to offer an explanation of first language acquisition, and may also be relevant to second language acquisition. Offering an alternative processing principle that cannot in fact explain the **acquisition** of an SVO order, though it might explain the **use** of it once it has been acquired, does not help to settle the issue of whether or not UG is still active in L2 acquisition.

Clahsen and Muysken argue that the L2 learner's assumption of SVO order is evidence against UG in L2 acquisition because if it is UG that causes L1 learners to assume SOV order for German, L2 learners ought to do the same, if UG were still available. However, there is a potential explanation of the initial assumption of SVO order which is consistent with the assumption that UG is still available to L2 learners. It relates to the fact that the Head-position Parameter usually operates consistently across syntactic categories, German being an exception in this respect. Suppose that the L2 learner assumes that the L2, like the L1, will show consistent head-position across categories,[13] and that the L2 learner is responsive to a number of properties of the L2 input but is misled by this assumption of consistency. The position of specifiers and complements in NPs and PPs in German is such as to suggest that German is head-initial. This plus the consistency assumption will be enough to yield VO order, even for the Turkish learners of German.[14] Furthermore, it will explain the acquisition of the SVO order, not just its use in production.

The claim that L2 learners adopt an incorrect word order for German is not in itself an argument against the operation of UG, since both SVO and SOV are possible word orders. Crucial for Clahsen and Muysken's argument that adult learners do not observe UG are the rules they use to describe the adult language in stages 3 and 4. They propose that the adult learner's inability to reset to SOV order leads to a number of unnatural rules, which are the result of trying to maintain SVO as the underlying order and yet handle the surface facts of German. They claim that adults in stage 3 have rules moving particles and non-finite verbs to the end of the sentence; in stage 4, a rule of subject-verb inversion is triggered by some topicalized element. Such rules would, for various technical reasons, count as unnatural in the GB framework. In contrast, the rule that they propose for L1 acquisition which moves the finite verb to the left is natural.

Notice that Clahsen and Muysken describe very similar acquisition data in one way for L1 learners and in another for L2. For example, in stage 3, sequences like S V^{+F} O V^{-F} are described as underlying SOV + a rule of verb second for L1 learners but as SVO + movement of non finite elements to the end for L2 learners. The L1 order A V^{+F} S in stage 3 is assumed to be the result of the finite verb moving into COMP and an adverb moving into the topic position. In L2 acquisition, on the other hand, the same sequence, produced in stage 4, is supposed to be the result of several unnatural permutations of elements.

Data are, of course, amenable to many different interpretations. Another theory consistent with these L2 data is that L2 learners are capable of resetting parameters, that they switch to head-final VPs at stage 3 (du Plessis et al. 1987; Schwartz and Tomaselli 1988). Then the natural leftward verb second rule and topicalization possibilities can be assumed to operate in L2 acquisition as well, removing any need to assume that L2 learners hypothesize unnatural rules.[15] What is in dispute here is not the data but how they are interpreted. In other words, the question of whether or not L2 learners adopt unnatural rules is not one that can be answered in isolation simply by looking at what they do. The important question is how one interprets what learners do, and this will depend on one's theory. Clahsen and Muysken's theory is that L2 learners of German maintain a D-structure word order of SVO at all stages; in that case unnatural rules will indeed result. But this is not the only theory consistent with the data drawn from L2 learners of German. It is perfectly consistent with the UG position to argue that L2 learners of German, although starting off with the incorrect value for the Head-position Parameter, in fact switch to the correct value at a later stage, thus obviating the need to describe their language in terms of unnatural rules.

4.6.3   *The Head-position Parameter: where are we now?*

L2 acquisition researchers have used the Head-position Parameter to make competing claims. Flynn argues that this parameter is available to L2 learners, that they are sensitive to the L2 head-position, although there is delay in acquiring properties that are affected by head-position (anaphora interpretation, according to her) when head-position differs in the L1 and L2. In contrast, Clahsen and Muysken argue that neither its L1 nor L2 value is available, and that difficulties in the L2 acquisition of German word order can be explained on this assumption.

As we have seen, there are some problems with the assumption that anaphora and word order are linked in the way that Flynn assumes, and her results do not strongly support such a link. On the other hand, Clahsen and Muysken's data are open to reinterpretation; an incorrect value of the parameter may be initially assumed by learners of German but subsequently reset.

Furthermore, even if one could demonstrate an obvious ability to reset from L1 to L2 head-position, or to acquire the L2 head-position without first assuming that of the L1, this would not necessarily count as useful evidence for UG. Those who argue that UG is no longer available to L2 learners could also argue that word order differences are often sufficiently obvious from the L2 input for it to be unnecessary to attribute any success in this area to the operation of innate principles or parameters.

Thus, the issue of whether the Head-position Parameter operates in L2 acquisition remains unresolved, and it may, in any case, not be possible to determine the status of UG in L2 acquisition using this parameter. We turn to some rather different examples in the next section, where the effects of parametric differences are more subtle.

4.7 The ECP and Subjacency revisited

Crucial to the argument that UG is still operating is the question of the ability to reset parameters. We have already seen some potential examples:

learners appear to be able to reset the Prodrop Parameter (at least from [−prodrop] to [+ prodrop]), and to reset the Head-position Parameter (on certain analyses). However, for both of these cases, it might be objected that the necessary information for the correct setting is explicitly available in the L2 input and thus the whole apparatus of UG is not required to explain successful acquisition; missing pronouns are 'obvious' in Spanish, as are word order differences, especially when the L2 is superficially a more consistent language than German. Thus, the acquisition of these properties of the L2 could be explained without having to assume the operation of UG parameters; the input does not underdetermine the final grammar, and no special mechanisms need be postulated.

What is required is the investigation of parameters whose effects are quite subtle, such that parametric differences would not be immediately obvious to a learner in the absence of the operation of UG. As Bley-Vroman (1989) points out, L2 learners should not be able to work out properties of the L2 which are underdetermined by the input data, if UG is no longer available to them. Alternatively, if L2 learners successfully arrive at the relevant properties of the L2 under such conditions, and these properties are not exemplified in the L1, then there is support for the claim that L2 learners rely on UG, rather than the L1 alone, to acquire complex and subtle properties of the L2.

In Chapter 3, several studies were considered which looked at the Empty Category Principle and Subjacency (Schachter 1988a, 1989b; Bley-Vroman et al. 1988). In these studies, the question of interest was whether learners with L1s in which these principles had not been activated would show evidence of observing them when acquiring an L2 in which they operate.

In this section, a different aspect of Subjacency and the ECP will be considered. Both principles have parameters associated with them. That is, there is some variation in the way these principles operate: languages which observe the ECP do not necessarily have the same proper governors, and languages which observe Subjacency do not necessarily have the same bounding nodes (see 1.8.2.4 and 1.8.2.8). Where the L1 and the L2 both observe Subjacency or the ECP but differ as to bounding nodes or proper governors, the effects of these parametric differences are sufficiently subtle for them not to be easily inducible from L2 input alone.

4.7.1   *The ECP and governing categories*

Differences between English and Dutch with respect to the operation of the Empty Category Principle (ECP) are relevant for investigating whether parameter resetting is possible in the absence of clear L2 input. As discussed in 1.8.2.8, there are differences in the behaviour of complementizers in English depending on whether an object or a subject in a lower clause is questioned, as can be seen in (9):

(9)   a.   Who do you think that Mary saw _?
　　 b.   Who do you think Mary saw _?
　　 c.   *Who do you think that _ saw Mary?
　　 d.   Who do you think _ saw Mary?

In (9a) and (9b), the *wh*-phrase, an object, can move out of the lower clause, and the complementizer *that* may be present or absent. (9d) shows that the *wh*-phrase can also move out when it is a subject; however, this is not possible if the complementizer remains in place, as in (9c). The ungrammaticality of (9c) is due to the ECP; proper government is blocked because the presence of *that* in COMP prevents the trace in COMP from c-commanding the subject trace (1.8.2.8).

The question that concerns us is whether L2 learners of English know the distinction between extractions of subjects and objects, particularly whether they know that sentences like (9c) are ungrammatical, when their L1, in this case Dutch, behaves differently with respect to these structures.

Let us first consider whether the English input is sufficient to make the ungrammaticality of (9c) obvious to the learner. The input might well contain sentences like (9a) and (9b), which would suggest that the presence of *that* is optional in English. This impression could be reinforced by other common English sentences like:

(10)   a.   This is the man that I met yesterday
　　 b.   This is the man I met yesterday
(11)   a.   I said that he could come
　　 b.   I said he could come

In other words, the positive evidence from English does not indicate any particularly difference between cases where *that* is retained and cases where it is omitted. If L2 learning proceeds only by means of inductive generalizations, the learner could reasonably assume that the occurrence of *that* is optional. The only indication that it is not always optional is the non-occurrence of forms like (9c). As we saw in Chapter 1, it is usually assumed in the learnability literature that it is impossible for learners to detect such non-occurrences without negative evidence (Berwick 1985; Wexler and Manzini 1987).

Could Dutch learners of English reconstruct the impossibility of *that* in sentences like (9c) on the basis of the L1? In Dutch, in contrast to English, an embedded subject can be extracted (Koopman 1984), leaving a complementizer next to the empty category, as in (12):

(12) *Wie   denk je   dat hem gisteren   gezien heeft?*
      Who think you that him yesterday seen   has
      'Who do you think saw him yesterday?'

The complementizer may not be deleted in these cases. The surface data in the L1 Dutch, then, do not appear to allow the L2 learner to work out the relevant properties of English. This difference between English and Dutch is accounted for by a parametric difference as to what categories they allow as proper governors. In Dutch but not English, COMP is a proper governor, and governs the trace of the moved subject, so that an ECP violation is not involved in these cases (du Plessis et al. 1987; Koopman 1984). This accounts for a wide range of phenomena in Dutch besides the one structure being discussed here.

If UG is not available and learners rely on their L1 for abstract properties of language, one would expect Dutch learners of English to assume that *that*-trace sequences are possible in English. If, on the other hand, UG is still fully reactivatable, then not only should ECP still be available, but also the possibility of detecting differences in the permissible proper governors allowed by different languages.

In a pilot study, Dutch learners of English were tested to see if they would treat extractions of subjects and objects differently in English (White 1987c). Sixty-two Dutch adults, at an advanced level, were tested. Thirty adult native speakers of English served as controls. The test was a preference task in which subjects were presented with pairs of English sentences, in written form. They were asked to compare the sentences and choose one of three responses: the first sentence seems better; the second sentence seems better; they seem the same. The sentence pairs contained identical vocabulary and structure, and differed only as to the presence or absence of the complementizer, which was found sometimes in the first sentence of the pair, sometimes in the second. Three of the sentence pairs were like (9a) and (9b), with extractions of objects, and six of the pairs were like (9c) and (9d), where subjects were extracted.

The reason for asking subjects to compare sentences, as opposed to making outright judgments about them, was that this would, presumably, reduce the influence of pragmatic factors or vocabulary, and force subjects to consider the syntactic structure of the sentences. Furthermore, asking subjects to express a preference is not open to the possibility that they might respond according to some response bias towards accepting or rejecting all sentences (see Chapter 3 for discussion). However, preference tasks lead to other problems. A preference is not a direct indication of grammatical competence, as we have already seen; subjects or native speakers could accept (or reject) both sentences in a pair and yet have a preference for one of them. Thus, the preference task results will indicate which sentences are preferred, but will not indicate whether the unpreferred sentences are in fact accepted or rejected.

Results are tabulated in Table 4.6 according to whether subjects preferred the sentence where *that* was retained (+ that) or the sentence where *that* was omitted (− that) or whether they thought both to be equally acceptable (same). The native speaker controls show a definite preference for *that* to be omitted, as predicted in cases of subject extraction and, somewhat unexpectedly, in cases of object extraction as well. There is a significant difference between the responses choosing the [− that] option for the two cases: 98% for extracted subjects versus 81% for extracted objects. This difference suggests that native speakers do indeed treat extraction of subjects differently from extraction of objects. However, here we see the disadvantage of not having an outright judgment task; one cannot tell whether the control group finds the sentences with *that* to be actually ungrammatical.

Table 4.6   Preference judgments from Dutch learners of English on subject and object extractions, in percentages (White 1987)

	Control group (n=30)			Dutch group (n=62)		
	+that	−that	Same	+that	−that	Same
Subjects	0	98.3	1.7	6	81	11.3
Objects	9	81	10	12.4	60.5	26.5

A similar differential treatment shows up in the L2 learners: they choose the [− that] option in 81% of cases of extraction of subjects and in 60.5% of cases of extraction of objects, a significant difference. It is this differentiality that does not appear to be obvious from the L2 input and that cannot be worked out on the basis of the way ECP operates in the L1. If they were simply making the generalization that English allows optional *that*-deletion, one would expect them to treat extracted subjects and objects alike. Assuming that this difference is not something that they were explicitly taught, these results suggest that Dutch L2 learners of English have unconscious knowledge of the relevant properties of English. In other words, UG is reactivatable when there are parametric differences, in this case between permissible proper governors, so that learners are not necessarily stuck with the L1 value (even though this may be what they start out with). What learners know about the L2 appears to be more than they could have induced directly from the input and more than they could have reconstructed via the L1 alone.

4.7.2 *Subjacency and bounding nodes*

Subjacency provides another example of subtle parametric variation which could not easily be worked out on the basis of the L1 grammar or the L2 input alone. If L2 learners show evidence of having discovered a parametric difference between the L1 and L2 in this domain, this again suggests that UG must be active.

Subjacency is a principle placing bounds on movement; it stipulates that any application of *move α* may not cross more than one *bounding node* at a time. The bounding nodes for English are NP, S and S′ (Chomsky 1981b; Sportiche 1981).[16] (13a) and (13c) are ungrammatical in English because the *wh*-phrase has crossed more than one bounding node. In (13a), the *wh*-word has been extracted out of a complex nounphrase, crossing an S′, an NP and an S, as shown in (13b). In (13c), the *wh*-object of the lower clause has been extracted from a so-called *wh*-island, crossing two Ss and S′. In (13e), *Wh*-extraction of the object from the embedded clause is possible since the COMP position at the front of S′ contains no *wh*-phrase; in that case, the *wh*-word passes through the COMP, avoiding a Subjacency violation, as shown in (13f). However, in sentences like (13c), this is not possible because the COMP is occupied by another *wh*-phrase.

(13) a. *What did Mary believe the story that John saw?
      b. What$_j$ [$_S$ did Mary believe [$_{NP}$ the story [$_{S'}$ that John saw t$_j$]]]
      c. *What did John wonder whether Mary would do?
      d. What$_j$ [$_S$ did John wonder [$_{S'}$ whether [$_S$ Mary would do t$_j$]]]
      e. What did John think that Mary would do?
      f. What$_j$ [$_S$ did John think [$_{S'}$ t$_j$ that [S Mary would do t$_j$]]]

There is parametric variation across languages in terms of the bound-ing nodes that they adopt. In particular, they differ as to the bounding status of S; Italian and French, for example, have NP and S' as bounding nodes, but not S (Chomsky 1981b; Rizzi 1982; Sportiche 1981). This means that in these languages certain extractions will be possible which are not possible in English. Equivalents of (13a) will still be ungrammatical because NP and S' are bounding nodes, and the *wh*-word has crossed both of these. Sentences similar to (13c) with extractions from *wh*-islands, on the other hand, will be grammatical in French and Italian, because only one bound-ing node, namely S', is crossed.

White (1985a, 1988a) investigates whether native speakers of French acquire knowledge of the status of S as a bounding node for Subjacency in English. French has fewer bounding nodes, allowing a wider range of per-missible extractions than English. The L1, therefore, cannot give precise evidence as to what kinds of extractions are possible in the L2. The positive L2 input is not transparent on this point either, since English allows a whole range of *wh*-movement structures. (The status of S as a bounding node is motivated by the non-occurrence of a range of structures, including sen-tences like (13c).)

White's (1988a) study included a native speaker control group and two groups of intermediate level adult learners of English, who were asked to perform a number of tasks, only one of which will be discussed here. This was a grammaticality judgment task which contained ungrammatical Subja-cency violations. Some, such as extractions from complex nounphrases, were ungrammatical in both French and English, whereas others, like extractions from *wh*-islands, were ungrammatical in English but not in French. Grammatical sentences were also included which served as a syntax test, in that they provided grammatical versions of structures of relevant complexity.

Results from the grammatical sentences indicated that the adult sub-jects had reached a level of sophistication in their interlanguage grammars such that any constraints relevant to extraction should be expected to operate. The results for the ungrammatical complex nounphrase and *wh*-island violations are presented in Table 4.7, in terms of an accuracy score. That is, these results represent the subjects' ability to identify a Subjacency violation as ungrammatical.

Table 4.7   Mean accuracy scores for ungrammatical Subjacency violations, in percentages (White 1988a)

	C	(1)	(2)
Complex NPs	96	80	81
Wh-islands	91	65	80

C=Control group (n=14), (1) = Ist adult group (n=18), (2) = 2nd adult group (n=17).

The native speakers of English reject the two kinds of Subjacency violations with a very high level of accuracy (over 90%). Both ESL groups also show considerable accuracy on the complex nounphrase violations (80% and over). These are the ones where parameter resetting is not at issue; they are ungrammatical in both languages. However, in the case of *wh*-island violations, there is a significant difference between the two experimental groups; only Group 2 achieves the level of accuracy that they achieved on the other ungrammatical sentences. These are the sentences where the bounding status of S may have effects. The results are consistent with the possibility that subjects initially assume that English, like French, does not have S as a bounding node (explaining the lower accuracy of Group 1 on these structures) and that they are eventually able to reset this parameter, so that S becomes bounding (explaining the greater accuracy of Group 2). If this is correct, it suggests that UG must have been involved, given that appropriate information about the bounding status of S is not available in the L1, and not easily inducible from the L2 input alone. (However, one problem with this interpretation is that the two groups performed very similarly on an independent measure of ESL competence (a cloze test); it is not clear why they should behave so differently with respect to the bounding status of S if their English is otherwise at a comparable level. However, teacher assessments suggest that the groups may in fact have been at different levels of proficiency: Group 2 was assessed as high intermediate, whereas Group 1 was assessed as low.)

4.8   Conclusion

In this chapter, the operation of parameters in second language acquisition has been discussed. Some of the evidence suggests that the L1 parameter setting is used by learners as an interim theory about the L2. In some cases, parameter resetting appears to be possible, even when the L1 grammar and the L2 data underdetermine the L2 setting, contrary to the claims of the UG-is-dead hypothesis. This suggests that UG is indeed reactivatable, a conclusion which was also supported by some of the studies discussed in Chapter 3. However, as only a few parameters have been investigated in the L2 acquisition context, this issue is by no means decided; research on other parameters is necessary, especially ones where the differences between the L1 and L2 are sufficiently subtle to allow one to rule out the L1 or general inductive strategies as a potential source of the L2 learner's knowledge.

4.9   Further reading

i.   A general justification of the application of parameters of UG to the study of L2 acquisition can be found in *Cook* (1985) and *White* (1988b).

ii.   *Hyams* (1986) investigates the operation of the Prodrop Parameter in L1 acquisition, and discusses the general implications of parameter theory for L1 acquisition, as do many of the papers in *Roeper and Williams* (1987). These works are quite technical, and may be difficult for those without much background in Government-Binding Theory.

iii.   *Flynn and O'Neil* (1988), *Pankhurst, Sharwood Smith and Van Buren* (1988) and *Gass and Schachter* (1989) contain a number of experimental studies investigating the role of parameters of UG in L2 acquisition.

Notes to Chapter 4

1.   In English, lexical subjects are not required in imperatives and in the second clause of a coordinate structure. These possibilities have nothing to do with the Prodrop Parameter.

2.   In fact, there are a number of prodrop languages which do not have rich inflectional systems at all, such as Japanese and Chinese. I will ignore these for the purposes of discussion here. See Jaeggli and Hyams (1988), Jaeggli and Safir (1989) who argue for a *Morphological Uniformity Hypothesis* which accounts for such languages as well as other prodrop languages.

3.   So-called because the subject of the embedded clause has been questioned, leaving a trace next to the complementizer. The *that*-trace effect is discussed in 1.8.2.8, in the context of the ECP. Various properties of [+ prodrop] languages allow the occurrence of *that*-trace sequences without an ECP violation. See Jaeggli (1982) and Rizzi (1982) for details.

4.   Liceras (1988b) studies speakers of [− prodrop] L1s learning a [+ prodrop] L2.

5.   See Liceras (1988b) for related observations and an experimental study of these issues.

6.   White (1989a) faced a similar problem in investigating English learners of French and French learners of English. A cloze test was adopted as the proficiency measure with French and English versions of the same passage.

7.   Lust and Flynn assume that Japanese, as a left-branching language, has a BA preference. In fact, this is not the case for pronominal anaphora. See, for example, O'Grady et al. (1986).

8.   This is another term for head position/branching direction.

9.   Bley-Vroman and Chaudron (1988) offer a detailed critique of Flynn's theory and methodology.

10.   Indeed, if Flynn (and Lust's) claims had originally been made in the context of a theory of anaphora, as opposed to a theory of word order, simple sentences involving reflexives would have shown that Japanese and English share many properties. In left-branching languages like Japanese, reflexives must be bound by a c-commanding antecedent, just as they must in a right-branching language like English. The Japanese equivalent of: *John despises himself* would be something like *John himself despises*. Although Japanese is left-branching, so that the object precedes the verb, it is also subject initial. Thus, in many structures involving grammatical anaphora, the direction of anaphora will necessarily be forwards.

11.   This position is also adopted by Clahsen (1988). Clahsen and Muysken (1989) have somewhat modified the claim that UG is not available; they now assume that principles are available but parameters are not. This will make no difference to the issues to be discussed here.

12.   Slobin and Bever's proposals are made for L1 acquisition, not L2. Clahsen and Muysken reject the canonical order strategy as an account of German L1 acquisition (a) because German L1 learners do not adopt SVO order and (b) because they recognize that the mixed orders in the German input raise considerable problems for this strategy. For some reason, they accept this as problematic for L1 learners, but not for L2.

13.   Head-position is consistent in the L1s of all the subjects discussed by Clahsen and Muysken.

14.   Clahsen and Muysken's account predicts that Dutch learners of German will assume underlying SVO order, even though Dutch shows the same word order variation as German. In contrast, the assumption that consistency across categories is involved allows for the possibility that Turks will choose SVO initially but that Dutch speakers would not. Since Dutch, like German, is inconsistent, the assumption of consistency would not be carried over from the L1.

15.   In fact, the picture is more complicated than this. Clahsen and Muysken offer a number of arguments against such reanalysis. See du Plessis et al. (1987) and Schwartz and

Tomaselli (1988) for counter-arguments. The discussion is highly technical, involving competing linguistic analyses of German.

16. Claims vary as to whether the parameter is S versus S' as the bounding node (Rizzi 1982), or both S and S' versus just S' (Chomsky 1981b; Sportiche 1981).

5 Markedness

5.1 Introduction

There are many different definitions of markedness, both within generative grammar and outside it. Most markedness theories attempt to account for structures which are exceptions to linguistic generalizations, or which are infrequent across the world's languages, or very complex. In addition, markedness has been used to make predictions about first and second language acquisition, the usual assumption being that marked properties of language are harder to learn than unmarked and will emerge later. Thus, there are two independent issues here: there is the question of the linguistic characterization of markedness and there is the question of the psycholinguistic correlates of markedness, such as this assumed difficulty and/or lateness of acquisition.

Many researchers argue that markedness is a relevant concept for explaining L2 acquisition, even though they do not accept markedness as defined in generative grammar, for example Kellerman (1979) for meaning, Eckman (1977) for phonology, and Gass (1979) and Hyltenstam (1984) for syntax. These researchers arrived at very similar ideas on the role of markedness to those discussed below, in most cases predating them, but at the same time assume very different definitions of markedness. They share the view, also adopted by most of the researchers discussed in this chapter, that unmarked structures have a special status in second language acquisition.

5.2 Markedness and core grammar in L1 acquisition

We shall concentrate on second language research that has adopted definitions of markedness from generative grammar. In particular, the research to be discussed in this chapter assumes a distinction between *core grammar* and peripheral phenomena. The fixed principles and open parameters of UG constitute the L1 learner's initial state. As the open parameters are fixed by the child on the basis of input from the language being learned, a core grammar results (Chomsky 1981a). A core grammar, then, is a particular instantiation of those principles and parameters that are built-in. Core grammars vary from language to language because not all the fixed principles are instantiated in all languages and because languages adopt different parameter settings. Core grammar is often thought of as unmarked because it is acquired with minimal evidence, or triggering data (see 1.9).

In contrast to this, there are properties of language that are not direct reflections of principles and parameters of UG; linguistic phenomena that are idiosyncratic, language specific, and exceptional are assumed to be outside of core grammar, forming a marked periphery, which varies considerably from language to language.

This distinction can be schematized as follows:

(1)

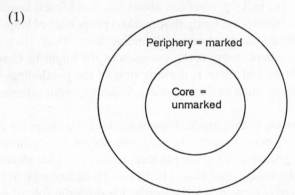

So far, one could simply defined markedness in terms of what is or is not present in UG. That is, any principles or parameters proposed in linguistic theory would be unmarked, whereas other linguistic structures would be marked. The acquisition correlates would be that core grammar is easier to acquire, because it is the result of triggering data interacting with built-in principles and parameters, whereas peripheral phenomena actually have to be learned.

However, the situation is not quite so straightforward. It appears that certain parameters have both an unmarked (U) and a marked (M) setting, as in (2):

(2)

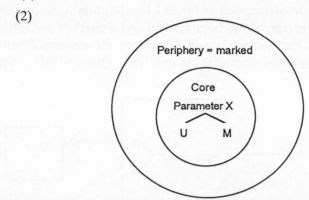

The idea is that certain parameters, rather than being truly open, have a preset initial, or unmarked, value. This is the value that L1 learners assume unless they encounter evidence to the contrary. In such circumstances, it is no longer possible to define markedness solely in terms of the contents of UG. Instead, it is assumed that the marked value of the parameter is the one which requires specific positive evidence. In Chapter 6, we shall consider in detail how to determine which value of a parameter fulfils this requirement, and how this relates to the assumption that negative evidence is not reliably available to L1 learners.

As a brief illustration, consider the principle of Subjacency. Bounding nodes for subjacency are parameterized (4.7.2). The more bounding nodes a language has, the fewer extractions are possible, because the bounding nodes restrict *wh*-movement. If we assume that UG is set up so that the unmarked value of this parameter is that all nodes are bounding, learners of languages where this is not the case will encounter positive evidence which indicates that they must reset the parameter in question. That is, they will encounter sentences where a *wh*-phrase has moved over certain nodes, suggesting that they cannot be bounding nodes. This positive evidence will motivate a marked parameter setting.

These two definitions of markedness assume that it is internal to the learner; markedness is a consequence of properties of UG. This contrasts with definitions found in the typological approach to linguistics (Comrie 1981; Greenberg 1966; Hawkins 1987), where markedness is defined externally, by looking at frequency of occurrence of various structures and at implicational relationships between certain structures in the languages of the world.

A fairly prevalent assumption as far as L1 acquisition is concerned is that if the target language allows both marked and unmarked variants[1] of some phenomenon, then acquirers will first adopt the unmarked before moving on to the marked (e.g. Hildebrand 1987; Phinney 1981; White 1982), as in (3):

(3)

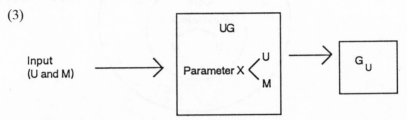

A stronger version of this hypothesis is proposed by Hyams (1986), who argues that the preset value of a parameter will be adopted even if this is *incorrect* for the language being acquired, i.e. even if there is no evidence in the target language for this value. In other words, something like (4) is assumed:

(4)

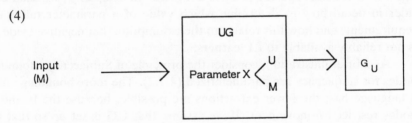

In fact, on current assumptions that a marked parameter setting is one which is motivated by positive evidence, both of these positions may be too strong. That is, if there is positive evidence in the input motivating a marked setting, it is not clear that the unmarked setting should necessarily constitute an acquisition stage before the marked one is acquired.

5.3 Markedness and L2 acquisition

There are at least three different ways in which the concept of markedness has been applied to second language acquisition, and all of these are also represented in work that takes generative grammar as its starting point. Markedness has been used to predict acquisition sequences (Mazurkewich), to account for language transfer (Liceras), and to predict directional differences, depending on which language is the L1 and which the L2 (Phinney). In all cases, the assumption is that unmarked properties will somehow prevail over marked, that the ILG will favour unmarked rules or parameter settings. Thus, Mazurkewich claims that an unmarked property in a given L2 will be acquired before its marked counterpart. Indeed, her position for L2 acquisition appears to be that unmarked forms will be found as an acquisition stage even if they are not in fact required in the target language. Liceras claims that unmarked aspects of the L1 will transfer rather than marked. Phinney claims that learning a language with the unmarked setting of a parameter will be easier than learning one with a marked setting.

5.4 Markedness and acquisition order

5.4.1 *Back to UG: unmarked before marked?*

In previous chapters, several positions as to the relationship between UG and second language acquisition have been outlined. One of these, the *pure UG* hypothesis, assumes that UG operates identically in L1 and L2 acquisition and that UG can interact directly with L2 input (2.6.1). This view is particularly relevant in the context of markedness. If L1 acquisition includes a developmental stage where unmarked structures or parameter settings are instantiated regardless of the actual situation in the target language, then the same would be predicted for L2 learners, on the assumption that the L2 learner reverts to the preset options of UG and tries these first. In addition, there should be no transfer of marked parameter settings or peripheral rules from the mother tongue. This is a strong hypothesis which has the potential to predict similarities across learners of different L1s (they all start off with unmarked settings) and similar acquisition sequences (unmarked before marked). Such assumptions underlie the work of Mazurkewich.

Mazurkewich (1984a,b) adopts the core/periphery distinction outlined above, where unmarked properties of language are identified with core grammar and marked properties with the periphery, as in Figure 1. Since she is not concerned with parameters, the question of the markedness status of different parameter settings does not arise. She argues that if the learner (L1 or L2) is acquiring a language with a marked structure, he or she will go through a stage of using the unmarked equivalent before the marked one is acquired. In other words, UG reverts back to preset options in L2 acquisition, and the learner's prior experience with the mother tongue (or any other non-native languages) has no effect. This predicts that all L2 learners will show the same developmental sequence of unmarked before marked, regardless of their L1.

Mazurkewich's hypothesis bears a resemblance to the natural order hypothesis of Krashen (1981) which tries to explain certain morpheme acquisition sequences by claiming that they are due to a natural order. However, it differs crucially in that specific predictions are made in advance of the data, based on the identification of structures as unmarked or marked, so that her hypothesis is empirically testable, in contrast to the natural order hypothesis which is entirely post hoc.

Mazurkewich identifies two English structures where both an unmarked and a marked variant are found. The first pair of structures are dative complements. English allows two complements with certain verbs, as in (5):

(5)   a.   John gave a book to Mary (NP PP = U)
       b.   John gave Mary a book   (NP NP = M)

The NP PP complement in (5a) is considered to be part of core grammar and unmarked whereas the NP NP structure in (5b), the double object structure, is marked. With some verbs, like *give* in (5a), the preposition is *to*; other verbs take *for*, for example *buy*. Mazurkewich looked at both types of verbs.

The second pair of structures she is concerned with are dative structures with questioned prepositional phrases. Again, English allows two possibilities, as in (6):

(6)   a.   To whom did John give a book?   (piedpiping = U)
       b.   Who(m) did John give a book to?   (preposition stranding = M)

Here, the structure in (6a) where the whole PP is fronted (piedpiping) is unmarked and the structure in (6b) where the preposition gets left behind (preposition stranding) is marked. Piedpiping and preposition stranding occur in other English structures as well, but Mazurkewich's investigation is confined to structures like (6). Although piedpiping is rare in English, Mazurkewich (along with many others) offers a range of arguments supporting the identification of piedpiping as the unmarked core structure.

In Mazurkewich's studies, English is the L2 and the L1s are French and Inuktitut.[2] French has only the unmarked version of the structures in question, and Inuktitut has nothing directly equivalent to either, it being a language of a very different type. The specific claim, then, is that native speakers of both French and Inuktitut will show an acquisition sequence for English of unmarked before marked for the structures in question.

Subjects were 45 French-speaking high school and college students (average age 18), and 38 Inuktitut-speaking high school students (average age 17). Mazurkewich also had two native speaker control groups, six 12 year olds and ten 15 year olds. Subjects were divided on the basis of a cloze test into three levels, beginner,[3] intermediate and advanced, the assumption being that the performance of the subjects at each level would reflect different points in an acquisition sequence. The French-speaking group's only exposure to English was via ESL instruction in the classroom, whereas the Inuktitut-speakers had received all their education in English.

The test on the dative complements is discussed in Mazurkewich (1984a). A grammaticality judgment task was used, which contained unmarked and marked structures like (5a) and (5b), as well as distractor sentences, to test her hypothesis that L2 learners would prefer the unmarked L2 structures like (5a) and would acquire these before the marked equivalents like (5b). Subjects were asked to indicate if a sentence was grammatical. A variety of different verbs was used; results are reported by grouping sentences into structural types. Table 5.1 reports the percentage of responses indicating that a given sentence type is grammatical. Since all the sentence types reported here are in fact grammatical, a response confirming that a sentence is grammatical is a correct response.

One can see from these results that the French-speakers do indeed prefer the unmarked structure, both in the case of *to* and *for* dative verbs. Furthermore, they seem to show a progression in the acquisition of the marked forms, with the weakest group least likely to accept these. Mazurkewich takes this as supporting her hypothesis that unmarked forms in the L2 emerge before marked. Unfortunately, however, this same result would be predicted on the basis of transfer, since French allows the unmarked but not the marked dative structure. Thus the results from the French speakers alone cannot tell us whether it is transfer or markedness that is at work.

Table 5.1   Dative structures — confirming responses, in percentages (Mazurkewich 1984a)

	Controls			French			Inuit	
	1	*2*	*B*	*I*	*A*	*B*	*I*	*A*
NP PP (to) (U)	100.0	100.0	98.4	94.3	96.0	96.7	97.5	100.0
NP NP (M)	90.0	100.0	47.9	62.9	81.3	80.0	87.5	87.8
NP PP (for) (U)	96.7	100.0	96.6	100.0	98.7	98.3	97.5	100.0
NP NP (M)	93.3	86.7	41.8	54.3	81.3	75.0	92.5	84.4

B=Beginners; I=Intermediate; A=Advanced

The results from the Inuktitut-speakers are therefore crucial and they are much less convincing for the markedness hypothesis. Mazurkewich does not report any statistical analyses on whether there are significant differences between the various groups[4] but the results suggest that although the Inuktitut-speakers accept unmarked structures more than marked, they are also very comfortable with the marked structures. Their judgments look very similar to those of the control groups and there is no evidence for an acquisition sequence within the marked sentence types.

The same subjects participated in a written question formation task (Mazurkewich 1984b) to test whether or not they would use marked preposition stranding, as in (6b), the prediction being that they would prefer unmarked piedpiping, as in (6a). Subjects were given declarative sentences, as in (8), with a phrase underlined which they were asked to question:

(8)   a.   Cathy gave a book *to Kevin*
      b.   Cathy gave *Kevin* a book

Results are reported in terms of whether they produced a correct, unmarked piedpiped question as in (9a), a correct, marked preposition stranding question as in (9b), or various errors, which Mazurkewich divides into different sub-types but which I will group together.

(9)   a.   To who(m) did Cathy give a book?
      b.   Who(m) did Cathy give a book to?[5]

In Table 5.2, results from a subset of the various sentence types discussed by Mazurkewich are reported.

It is quite clear from the high proportion of errors that this question formation task caused problems for all subjects, particularly the native

Table 5.2   Question formation — Distribution of responses, in percentages
(Mazurkewich 1984b)

| | Controls | | | French | | | Inuit | |
	1	*2*	*B*	*I*	*A*	*B*	*I*	*A*
NP PP (to)								
marked	76.6	53.4	5	14.3	18.7	46.7	42.5	49.5
unmarked	16.7	43.3	27	22.9	40.0	11.6	17.5	25.8
errors	6.7	3.3	68	62.8	41.3	41.7	40.0	24.7
NP NP								
marked	83.3	66.6	4.3	5.7	16.0	33.3	62.5	40.4
unmarked	6.7	20.0	14.1	8.6	18.7	8.3	12.5	18.0
errors	10.0	13.4	81.6	85.7	65.3	58.4	25.0	41.6
NP PP (for)								
marked	70.0	63.3	5.9	2.9	12.0	36.6	55.0	39.4
unmarked	16.7	36.7	30.7	28.6	42.7	10.0	15.0	25.8
errors	13.3	0	63.4	68.5	45.3	53.4	30.0	34.8
NP NP								
marked	76.6	70.0	3.4	5.7	9.4	41.6	62.5	41.6
unmarked	6.7	16.7	14.7	11.4	21.4	5.0	7.5	21.4
errors	16.7	13.3	81.9	82.9	69.2	53.4	30.0	37.0

B=Beginners; I=Intermediate; A=Advanced

speakers of French. It is also clear that only the French speakers perform as predicted on correctly formed questions. For all sentence types (including ones not reported in Table 5.2), the French-speakers produce more unmarked questions than marked but the Inuktitut-speakers produce more marked questions than unmarked. This is true both when the stimulus declarative sentences contained a preposition (as in (8a)) and when they did not (as in (8b)). Once again, we suffer from not having statistical analyses of the data but, if anything, it looks as if the Inuktitut-speakers are learning the **unmarked** forms (i.e., there appears to be a gradual increase in production of these with increasing level).

Although Mazurkewich argues that these results support her hypothesis that L2 learners will learn unmarked before marked, this is not the case. The behaviour of the native speakers of French is consistent with their carrying over the unmarked structures from their L1, and thus cannot tell us whether L2 learners revert to core grammar. The native speakers of Inuktitut clearly prefer to form questions with preposition stranding, the peripheral structure. As they had received all their education in English, it is possible that at the time of testing they had had too much exposure to English for the unmarked option to prevail any longer. Their results certainly do not show a current preference for the unmarked structure and we simply do not know how they would have behaved had they been tested after less exposure to the L2.

This raises another problem in the context of the preposition stranding, which is that it is very frequent in English, even if technically marked. In other words, there is ample positive evidence to override the unmarked piedpiping here. Any L2 learner is likely to come across stranding in the input, and, if anything, the marked structure is more likely to be used in conversation than the unmarked. Indeed, it is not at all clear that children learning English as their mother tongue in fact show the predicted order of unmarked before marked. Experimental evidence suggests that young children either have a preference for marked stranding over unmarked piedpiping or else acquire them together (French 1985; Krause and Goodluck 1983). In a study which extends Mazurkewich's work to other English preposition stranding structures (i.e., relative clauses) and to native speakers of other languages, Bardovi-Harlig (1986) found that stranding was invariably acquired before piedpiping and she suggests that this is due to the salience of the former in the input.

It seems that the pure UG hypothesis which claims that there will be an acquisition sequence of unmarked before marked cannot be maintained for L2 acquisition on the basis of Mazurkewich's results. As we have seen, the pure UG hypothesis assumes no L1 influence because UG reverts to its preset options. In Mazurkewich's studies, the unmarked structure was also the only possibility allowed in the L1 in the case of the French-speakers. As a result, we are unable to determine the cause for their preference for unmarked structures, i.e., whether it was due to the influence of the L1 or to the emergence of a core grammar. The fact that the Inuktitut-speakers behaved differently suggests that the L1 was indeed having an influence on the French-speakers.

5.4.2 *Marked and unmarked together*

Another way of testing the pure UG hypothesis which is not open to this problem is to take a situation where the L1 has a **marked** parameter setting or a peripheral rule. The pure UG hypothesis predicts that the marked L1 value should not transfer and that the learner will immediately adopt the unmarked value in the L2, both in the case where it is appropriate for the L2 and in the case where it is not. With this logic in mind, White (1987b) looked at the reverse situation of the one that Mazurkewich studied. Native speakers of English learning French were studied, using the same kinds of structures as those used by Mazurkewich, i.e. dative complements and questioned prepositional phrases, in a variety of grammaticality judgment tasks, to see whether subjects would assume the marked double object structure and marked preposition stranding to be possible in French, where both are ungrammatical. The pure UG hypothesis predicts that learners should reject these structures in French. White's subjects were quite accurate in rejecting preposition stranding in French but were much more inclined to accept the double object structure. The latter results suggests that the pure UG hypothesis cannot be maintained, since it can account for the rejection of stranding but not for the failure to reject double object complements.

In fact, the strongest test of the pure UG hypothesis would be to take a situation where both the L1 and the L2 allow only the marked structure. In this situation, neither L1 structures nor L2 input would motivate the choice of unmarked, so that if the unmarked forms showed up in the ILG, this would be strong evidence in favour of the hypothesis that UG can override both the L1 and marked forms of L2 input. As far as I know, no study of this type has been done but one which gets close to it is Van Buren and Sharwood Smith (1985). They take Dutch as the L1 and English as the L2. This fits the above requirement in that both languages allow the marked preposition stranding, although stranding is much more constrained in Dutch than it is in English. It departs from the above ideal in that both languages also allow the unmarked piedpiping, so that effects of transfer or L2 input cannot be eliminated.

In a pilot study of Dutch school children and university students, Van Buren and Sharwood Smith included a task in which subjects were given a sentence with an unplaced preposition and asked to indicate where the preposition could go, as in Figure 5.1.

The test, which contained five items, was taken by 27 school children, who had had one year of English instruction, and 46 students in their second or third year of studying English at university. Results are shown in

Sample test item	Sample response
What did you stand on	What did you stand on *and* On what did you stand (i.e. the subject allows both stranding and pied piping)

Figure 5.1   Sample test item (Van Buren and Sharwood Smith 1985)

Table 5.3. Given the proportion of responses which made use of only preposition stranding or both preposition stranding and piedpiping, it is clear that both groups by no means exclude marked structures in the L2; rather, both marked and unmarked forms are used, again suggesting that the pure UG hypothesis cannot be maintained.[6] However, the university students were certainly not beginners and most subjects would have had exposure to English outside the classroom, so it is possible that they had already passed a stage of preferring unmarked forms.

Table 5.3   Types of responses, in percentages (Van Buren and Sharwood Smith 1985)

	Only piedpiping	Only stranding	Both
School	38	32	24
University	12	36	48

5.5 Markedness and transfer

5.5.1 *Transfer of the unmarked value?*

The studies discussed above have yielded mixed results. The hypothesis that L2 learners revert to core grammar and show an acquisition sequence of unmarked before marked is not supported by the experimental evidence. Mazurkewich's claim was that unmarked structures or parameter settings would be preferred regardless of the values realized in the L1. An alternative possibility is that language transfer takes place and that it is influenced by markedness. This is the position to be reviewed in this section.

Most researchers who have assumed a relationship between markedness and transfer have argued that unmarked aspects of the L1 will be more liable to transfer than marked. The idea is that L2 learners are still sensitive to marked properties of their L1s and will not consider them transferable to the L2 (Kellerman 1979, 1983). This is the position taken by Liceras (1985, 1986). Mazurkewich's results could be reinterpreted as supporting transfer of unmarked forms, although this is not her position. That is, one can replace Mazurkewich's argument that the unmarked emerges first because UG is reset to preset values with an argument that unmarked structures from the L1 are transferred to the L2. This would explain the behaviour of the native speakers of French in her experiments. However, White's findings that English learners of French transfer the marked double object structure from English would not fit with this view of transfer.

Liceras (1985, 1986) seeks to identify factors which influence the form of interlanguages. She argues that properties of the L1 and the L2, as well as markedness, must all be taken into account and that unmarked aspects of language are more likely to show up in the interlanguage than marked. Liceras's study is a detailed examination of many aspects of the L2 acquisition of Spanish relative clauses, and related structures. Here, we shall focus only on her claims about the effects of the L1; she suggests that unmarked properties of the L1 will be likely to transfer into the ILG. She assumes that learners have intuitions about marked structures in the L1 and are able to detect if the L2 does not have these marked structures.

Like Mazurkewich, Liceras's study includes (but is not confined to) piedpiping and preposition stranding; she also identifies preposition stranding as a peripheral phenomenon, i.e., outside of core grammar. In Liceras's work, the L1 (English) has both the unmarked and marked structures, and the L2 (Spanish) has only the unmarked one. This allows her to test the role of markedness in transfer: if only unmarked forms transfer, as she predicts, then one does not expect marked L1 forms to show up in the interlanguage. She thus predicts that native speakers of English learning Spanish will not assume that Spanish allows preposition stranding, because it is marked.

Liceras studied 45 adult learners of Spanish, divided into three equal groups: beginners, intermediate and advanced. They were all native speakers of English. All had also studied French, and some knew Italian or Portuguese. This other language knowledge is potentially problematic, in that French, Italian and Portuguese share the prohibition against preposition stranding, so that if L2 learners of Spanish reject it, one cannot be sure that this is because of something they have noticed about Spanish, or because it is something they have learned with respect to their other non-native languages. She had a small control group of 5 native speakers of Spanish.

Subjects' knowledge of piedpiping and preposition stranding was tested with a translation task and a grammaticality judgment task. Subjects were asked not only to judge sentences but also to correct and translate them, so as to ensure that the relevant properties of the sentences were being judged. There were only two preposition stranding sentences in the judgment task so results must be interpreted with caution. The beginners were much more likely to accept stranding than the intermediate and advanced groups. 43% of the beginners' responses to the stranding sentences were acceptances, in contrast to 4% for the intermediate group and 3% for the advanced group. In the translation task, the same trend was apparent, but to a lesser extent. There were six preposition stranding sentences to be translated from English to Spanish. 20% of the beginners' translations of these made use of stranding in the L2, in contrast to 1% for the intermediate group and 1% for the advanced group. These results suggest that, contrary to Liceras's claim, the early interlanguage grammar is influenced by marked structures from the L1; however, her claim that marked L1 structures are not persistent is supported. Whether this is because learners can detect non-occurrence of the marked form in the L2 is still an open question. The beginners were the only group which had not received explicit instruction on the structures in question, so it is possible that the other groups had explicitly been taught not to strand.

Many of the other properties of the interlanguage grammar studied by Liceras relate to the complementizer system, which she looks at within the framework of filters proposed within earlier versions of generative grammar (Chomsky and Lasnik 1977; Baker 1979a). These filters have largely been superseded by the principles and parameters of GB theory. They were in some sense the precursors of parameters, and the logic behind them (particularly the markedness logic) is still maintained in GB theory, so that L2 acquisition research conducted within this framework is still of considerable relevance to the issues being pursued here.

Chomsky and Lasnik (1977) argue that UG includes a universal set of filters which specify that certain sequences are prohibited (in other words, these are negative constraints, like other principles of UG). Since some languages observe these prohibitions and others do not, the possibility of variation must be built in. This is done by assuming that the prohibiting filters have two settings, *on* and *off*. Filters are preset to on and they can be switched off if input from the language being learned suggests that this must be so. In other words, there is an unmarked initial setting, and the marked setting is motivated by positive evidence, as is the case with certain parameters. An example is the *that-trace filter*, which has subsequently been subsumed under the ECP (1.8.2.8). The filter is preset at on, thus prohibiting structures of the form of (10):

(10)   *Who do you think that _ will win?

In languages like Dutch, as we have already seen, sentences equivalent to (10) are grammatical; these would provide positive evidence that this filter is switched off in that language.

One of the filters that Liceras is particularly concerned with is the empty complementizer (COMP) filter in (11), which disallows an empty COMP [e] in various structures:

(11)   *[e]

This filter is on in Spanish; it is off in English. In other words, Spanish relative clauses require the presence of a complementizer, whereas in English the complementizer is optional, as can be seen in (12) and (13); the same is true of embedded complements, as can be seen in (14) and (15). Sentences like (13b) and (15b) in English provide the necessary positive evidence to switch the filter off (i.e., to set it to its marked value).

(12)   a.   Ese chico francés *que* conoc ayer ....
       b.   *Ese chico francés conoc ayer ....
(13)   a.   That French man *that* I met yesterday...
       b.   That French man I met yesterday...
(14)   a.   La radio dice *que* la lucha es feroz
       b.   *La radio dice la lucha es feroz
(15)   a.   The radio says *that* the fighting is ferocious
       b.   The radio says the fighting is ferocious

Since *[e] represents the unmarked case, Liceras's claim is that native speakers of English learning Spanish will not transfer the marked possibility of empty COMPs from English to Spanish. The results from her judgment task were as follows: 49% of the beginners' responses, 25% of the intermediate and 9% of the advanced group were acceptances of empty COMPs, suggesting that the marked setting of the filter was operating in the early IL. Her hypothesis was better supported by the translation task: where the English stimulus sentence to be translated into Spanish included an empty COMP, subjects nevertheless supplied a complementizer in Spanish. Only 8% of the responses of the beginner and the intermediate groups gave sentences with empty COMPS, and only 1% of the advanced group's responses were of this type. We will return to this discrepancy between the results of the different tasks in 5.5.3.

5.5.2   Difficulty in acquiring marked L2 values?

In the above studies, Liceras hypothesized that marked properties of the L1 would be unlikely to show up in the ILG. This claim is only partially borne out by her data. A corollary is that when the L1 contains an unmarked setting of a filter and the L2 requires a marked one, the learner should have difficulty in acquiring the marked value and should be inclined to transfer the unmarked L1 value to the ILG. A pilot study by Adjémian and Liceras (1984), again focussing on relative clauses, is relevant in this context. They look at various structures, including the same *[e] filter discussed above, and they include cases where the L1 has the filter on (i.e., the unmarked setting) and L2 has it off (the marked setting), as well as the opposite situation.[7] In this study, there were 40 subjects, native speakers of English learning French or Spanish and native speakers of French learning English or Spanish. French is like Spanish in prohibiting empty COMPs. That is, French and Spanish are unmarked with respect to the filter whereas English is marked.

Subjects were all in first level language courses at the University of Ottawa, Canada, and had not been taught the structures in question. Subjects were given a variety of tasks: imitation, translation from L1 to L2 and from L2 to L1 (the latter both oral and written), and judgments (including correction). Here we will look only at the results from the English learners of French and the French learners of English, in three of the tasks. These are given in Table 5.4.

The results from the native speakers of English are similar to those found by Liceras for English-speaking learners of Spanish; empty COMPs are found but not extensively. If anything, these results offer stronger support for the hypothesis that only unmarked properties will transfer. Subjects imitate empty COMPs in the repetition task (40%), reject them totally in the judgment task, and use them occasionally (20%) in the translation task. Their fairly high level of occurrence in the repetition task may not reflect their competence at all. It can probably be attributed to conscienti-

Table 5.4   Responses to COMPs in restrictive relatives, in percentages (Adjémian and Liceras 1984)

	Repetition	Judgments	Written Translation
English - French			
Empty	40	0	20
Not empty	20	100	80
No response	20	0	0
French - English			
Empty	65.5	75	41
Not empty	6.4	25	59
No response	28.1	0	0

ous imitation on the part of subjects, since they were asked (as is usual in such tasks) to try and imitate the sentence as accurately as possible. Although imitation tasks are usually assumed to reflect a subject's interim competence (see Chapter 4), it is possible that short sentences can be imitated exactly as heard, even if the subject considers them ungrammatical, i.e., that subjects do not adjust short sentences to fit with the current grammar.

The results from the native speakers of French, on the other hand, suggest that the unmarked French value of the filter does not have such an influence that it leads to the exclusion of the marked L2 value. The French-speakers seem quite well aware that English allows marked empty COMPs. These are repeated (65.5%), judged acceptable (75%), and used in translation (41%). As Adjémian and Liceras suggest, these learners appear to be paying attention to properties of the L2 input. But notice that they are doing this despite the fact that this structure is marked in Liceras's terms, and despite the fact that the L1 requires an unmarked setting for this filter.

5.5.3 *Competence versus performance and task variability*

A few comments are in order here on the apparent variability of the subjects' performance on different tasks. A number of researchers (Ellis 1986; Tarone 1988) have argued that such variability must be accommodated within a theory of competence; that is, since performance varies, it must be represented within a theory of linguistic competence. This is not possible on the view that we are assuming, where competence represents only the linguistic knowledge internalized by the native speaker or the language learner. Many other factors may dictate how this competence is actually used but these factors do not rightly belong in a theory of linguistic competence but rather in a theory of linguistic performance (see Gregg 1989, Sharwood Smith, to appear, for further discussion).

A competence/performance distinction can account for some of the task differences found by Liceras (1985, 1986) and Adjémian and Liceras (1984). In the situations they studied, the marked forms are optional; that is, a language allowing a marked structure also allows the equivalent unmarked one. Certain tasks will offer the learner the opportunity to use either the unmarked form or the marked form. It is possible that a learner's linguistic competence might include both marked and unmarked forms but that he or she might prefer the unmarked form. Some tasks give a learner a greater opportunity to exercise such preferences: a translation task, for example, allows some leeway in how a particular structure is to be translated. Other tasks are intended as a means of forcing preferences to be set aside: in a judgment task, learners are asked what is in general possible, rather than what they would prefer to use on a particular occasion. Thus, certain tasks may give the impression of supporting a hypothesis more than others; the tasks where the subjects had some choice as to what structures to use suggest that there is indeed a preference for unmarked forms, but the tasks which force a decision about marked forms suggest that these are not excluded from the ILG.

To illustrate this point, consider the results from Adjémian and Liceras on the acquisition of English empty COMPs by native speakers of French, a language which does not allow them. In the judgment task, learners are asked to indicate whether sentences with empty COMPs are acceptable, and this they do — 75% of empty COMPs were judged acceptable, suggesting that they are aware of this property of English, that it is part of their competence. In the translation task, the use of empty COMPs is lower (41%), and the repetition task falls between the two (65.5%). Since English actually allows both empty and filled COMPs, linguistic competence will have to include this fact and this is done by assuming an optional rule of COMP deletion.[8] This rule allows (but does not require) material in COMP to be deleted. It does **not** specify what factors will lead to the application of the rule. Native speakers sometimes use it and sometimes do not, and the same appears to be true of these learners. In the judgment task, learners are forced to make a decision about sentences that they might not themselves produce, and they show a high level of acceptance of empty COMPs. In the translation task, there is some leeway in that translations with or without complementizers will be grammatical, and subjects chose sometimes to omit the complementizer (41%) and sometimes to use it (59%). This behaviour suggests that they have an optional rule of complementizer deletion, and also that they do not always use it, just like native speakers. The repetition task suggests the same thing; given a stimulus sentence with an empty COMP, subjects usually but not invariably repeat it with an empty COMP. Similar remarks apply to Liceras's study of native speakers of English learning Spanish, where empty COMPs were accepted in the judgment task but only infrequently used in the translation task, suggesting that their interlanguage may have (incorrectly) included an optional COMP-deletion rule which they did not necessarily use all the time.

Liceras's hypotheses are to be welcomed because she attempts to integrate properties of the L1, the L2, and markedness theory, i.e., she recognizes that many different influences interact in second language acquisition. It seems, however, that there are problems in using markedness to predict when transfer will and will not occur, just as there were problems with using it to predict acquisition sequences. Despite Liceras's predictions, marked properties did transfer, especially in early stages. Unmarked properties sometimes failed to transfer, and marked properties of the L2 input were taken into account. In the next chapter, we shall consider how to accommodate the fact that marked properties of language are not totally excluded from the ILG.

5.6 Markedness and directionality

The hypotheses that Mazurkewich and Liceras explore in terms of the core/periphery distinction could equally well be applied to parameters. For example, Mazurkewich's claim that unmarked structures will be acquired by L2 learners before marked ones is equivalent to saying that L2 learners will first adopt the unmarked setting of a parameter, regardless of whether this is the setting required in the L2, and regardless of the setting in their L1. Liceras's hypothesis that unmarked aspects of language are more likely to show up in the interlanguage is equivalent to saying that an unmarked parameter setting is more likely to transfer than a marked one.

In this section, claims relating to unmarked and marked parameter values will be considered, particularly the prediction of differences that depend on the markedness values of a parameter in the L1 and the L2. Claims in this area have centered on the Prodrop Parameter (see Chapter 4).

Phinney (1987) follows Hyams (1986) in assuming that [+ prodrop] is the initial value of the parameter. It should be noted that Hyams bases this claim on the behaviour of children learning English as their mother tongue; they go through a stage of systematically omitting subject pronouns before they begin to use them as required by English. Hyams (1986) specifically dissociates the initial value from markedness questions.[9] Phinney, however, assumes that [+ prodrop] is unmarked and [− prodrop] marked.

Like Mazurkewich and Liceras, Phinney assumes a special status for unmarked structures in second language acquisition. She differs from Mazurkewich in assuming that the L1 value of a parameter will be transferred, and she differs from Liceras in assuming that this will be true of both marked and unmarked parameter settings. Her directionality claim is that it will be easier for a learner to switch from a marked L1 to unmarked L2 than from an unmarked L1 to marked L2, on the assumption that a marked L2 value will be harder to acquire because it requires additional positive evidence to motivate it. In other words, she predicts, firstly, that native speakers of Spanish will initially treat English as if it is [+ prodrop] and that native speakers of English will initially treat Spanish as if it is [− prodrop]. Secondly, native speakers of English will reset the parameter to the Spanish value with less difficulty or sooner than native speakers of Spanish will reset to the English value, on the assumption that the English value is the marked one.

Phinney's data (discussed in 4.5) suggest that this prediction is correct. She found that native speakers of Spanish learning English failed to supply the pleonastic pronoun subject *it* and *there* in their written compositions, whereas English-speaking learners of Spanish correctly used null subjects in impersonal constructions.

Although these results suggest that it is easier to reset from the English value of the Prodrop Parameter to the Spanish value than vice versa, these data can also be accounted for by theories that assume that the Spanish value is the marked one and English the unmarked. White (1985c, 1986b), for example, argues that the [+ prodrop] value is marked, a position also shared by Berwick (1985), Rizzi (1986). This claim is based on a consideration of the kind of evidence needed to set parameters. [− prodrop] languages require lexical pronouns, whereas [+ prodrop] languages allow both null and lexical pronouns. If [− prodrop] is the initial, unmarked value, this can be reset to [+ prodrop] on the basis of simple positive evidence in the form of sentences with null subjects. White (1986b) argues that where the L1 has an unmarked value and the L2 requires a marked value, the marked L2 value will be motivated by the positive L2 data. Thus it will be obvious to an L2 learner on the basis of simple sentences that Spanish allows subjects to be omitted, and the relative ease with which English-speaking learners of Spanish acquire the [+ prodrop] setting is not surprising, even if [+ prodrop] is considered marked.

Although the claim that there are directional differences receives some justification from the prodrop data, we are in the unfortunate position of not knowing the source of the differences. The merits of the "unmarked → marked is harder than marked → unmarked" claim can only be assessed with reference to a parameter where there is no disagreement as to which value is the unmarked one. Phinney suggests that the same L2 data can be used to decide which setting is the marked one but this is not so. The data have to be interpreted within the context of a theory and, as we have seen, the data are consistent with two radically different hypotheses. Choosing between them will depend on additional data and/or developments in the theory. Indeed, a number of researchers have suggested recently that the Prodrop Parameter may not have a marked and unmarked value at all. In that case, directional differences will not be predicted for this parameter in L2 acquisition, and the differences that have been found with respect to use of null subjects remain unexplained in this framework.

5.7 Conclusion

The moral of this chapter might seem to be that one should abandon markedness as a useful concept for investigating second language acquisition. I should like to draw a different conclusion. What we are witnessing here is developing theories being applied to a particular domain. These theories may turn out to be right or wrong, but either way they generate specific predictions and can be further refined and extended, suggesting other analyses of what is going on in second language acquisition.

In this chapter, we have looked at a number of different positions on the role of markedness, as defined in generative grammar. All three views have taken as the null hypothesis the assumption that unmarked aspects of language have a special status and have sought to demonstrate this with L2 acquisition data. According to Mazurkewich, unmarked structures emerge earlier than marked; according to Liceras, they are more likely to transfer to the ILG; according to Phinney, they are easier to acquire. We have also seen that these claims are not at all clearly supported by the experimental evidence: marked properties are not excluded to the extent that these views predict. In the next chapter, we shall introduce another definition of markedness, also prevalent in generative grammar. This definition leads to somewhat different predictions for second language acquisition, in particular that unmarked rules or parameter settings no longer necessarily have the special status that has been accorded to them.

5.8 Further reading

i.   The relationship between markedness and transfer is discussed by *Kean* (1986), *White* (1986b, 1987b), *Zobl* (1983).

ii.   A number of papers in *Flynn and O'Neil* (1988) are concerned with markedness. The papers by *Mazurkewich* and by *Liceras*, for example, provide more recent versions of their hypotheses, as well as new data.

Notes to Chapter 5

1.   This is possible because in many cases, a marked structure or parameter setting includes its unmarked equivalent. This issue will be discussed further in Chapter 6.

2.   Inuktitut is a language spoken by the Inuit (Eskimo) of Canada.

3.   As none of the subjects were in fact beginners, a more appropriate classification for this group would have been *low*.

4.   See Kellerman (1985) for further discussion.

5.   Subjects were told that it did not matter whether they used *who* or *whom*.

6.   In other tests, subjects were more likely to accept piedpiping, but preposition stranding was not totally rejected.

7.   In fact, they consider the issue in terms of various reformulations of the filters proposed by Baker (1979a); for ease of exposition, I have recouched the issue in terms of the Chomsky and Lasnik filters.

8.   In other words, in languages where the *[e] filter is off, one still has to account for the fact that both empty and filled COMPs are possible, hence this optional rule.

9.   She considers that [+prodrop] emerges first for independent reasons, not because it is the unmarked value of a parameter (see Hyams 1986, Chapter 6).

6 Learnability and the Subset Principle

6.1 Positive and negative evidence, and learning principles

The language learner's task is to come up with a grammar which accounts for the input, and which allows the learner to understand and produce language. There are two kinds of evidence that can potentially serve as input to a grammar. *Positive evidence* indicates what is possible in the target language; it consists of utterances which the learner is exposed to. *Negative evidence* indicates what is not possible; it consists of information about ungrammaticality, as found, for example, in error correction or grammar teaching.

In Chapter 1, we saw that the assumption of an innate UG is motivated by a number of factors, including the lack of reliable and specific negative evidence to L1 learners (1.4.3). UG removes the need for at least some kinds of negative evidence in the following way: it provides a blueprint as to what languages can be like, preventing the L1 learner in advance from making certain assumptions. In other words, the types of hypotheses entertained by the child are constrained via UG; certain kinds of ungrammatical structures are ruled out in advance without any need for negative evidence; certain logical possibilities are never entertained and so the question of what kind of evidence might remove them is no longer at issue. For example, a principle like Subjacency prevents movement out of certain configurations, so that children do not have to learn of the impossibility of sentences like:

(1)   *What did John believe the claim that Mary saw _?

However, even given the existence of principles of UG, it is still possible in principle for the child to arrive at incorrect hypotheses for the target language. These hypotheses must at some point be disconfirmed if the child is to attain an adult-like grammar, and the question arises as to how they can be disconfirmed with positive evidence only, on the assumption that negative evidence is not available.

To illustrate the problem, we will look at three different kinds of incorrect hypotheses and consider how they can be 'unlearned'; the first two can be removed via positive evidence but the third appears to require negative evidence. These examples do not depend on UG, but we shall see subsequently that the same issues arise in the context of parameters.

The first kind of incorrect hypothesis involves under-representation. Assume a first language learner, with an internalized grammar X. Grammar Y represents the grammar of the language being learned. When some aspect of the input is not accommodated in X and is accommodated in Y, grammar X is less general than grammar Y, in the sense that it under-represents the input. Positive evidence can bring about change from X to Y. This circumstance is diagrammed in (2):

(2)

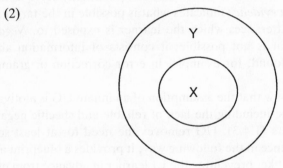

As an example, consider the acquisition of the complements of verbs. A verb like *see* can take a direct object noun phrase or a sentential complement, as in (3a) and (3b):

(3)   a.   Mary saw John
      b.   Mary saw that John was tired

Learners do not necessarily acquire all the complements of a particular verb at once. A learner at stage X might already know that *see* takes a direct object noun phrase but not yet know that it can also take a sentential complement. When this learner notices sentences like (3b) in the input, these provide positive evidence that an addition must be made to the lexical entry for *see*, to accommodate the fact that this verb takes both complements. Once this information is entered, the learner has a different grammar, Y, which represents an addition to X.

A second type of incorrect hypothesis requires that a form or rule in one grammar be replaced by something else, as illustrated in (4):

(4)

Certain kinds of overgeneralization fall into this category. Suppose, for example, that the learner is forming all English past tenses totally regularly, by the addition of the morpheme /-ed/, resulting in overgeneralizations such as *bringed* and *runned*. These forms can be disconfirmed by positive evidence of the existence of the alternate forms: *brought* and *ran*. That is, the positive evidence contains instances of the correct, irregular forms. The learner could change from grammar X (the one having an overgeneral past tense rule) to Y (the one that recognizes exceptional forms) with positive evidence only.

A potential problem in cases like (4) is that learners might think that they are in a situation like (2). For instance, they might think that *brought* or *ran* represents an additional past tense form, as opposed to being the only possible form. Many researchers therefore suggest that learners are guided by a Uniqueness Principle, which says that any particular semantic concept will have only one syntactic or morphological realization (Berwick 1985; Pinker 1984; Wexler 1981). Thus, for any particular verb, past tense can only be realized by one affix. This means that when the learner notices forms like *brought* or *ran*, the Uniqueness Principle will force them to recognize these as replacements for *bringed* and *runned*. (Notice that negative evidence could in principle play the same role as positive evidence plus the Uniqueness Principle here. That is, one could correct a learner who says *bringed* by informing him that he should not say *bringed* but *brought*. However, as discussed in Chapter 1, we cannot assume that L1 learners regularly get such explicit correction.[1])

The third case represents a more problematic kind of overgeneralization. Suppose that X (the earlier grammar) contains forms or rules which are incorrect for Y, as shown in (5), and which must be eliminated. This differs from (4), in that the form or rule that must be eliminated will not be replaced by something else.

(5)

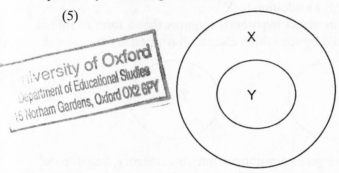

As an example, consider the sentences in (6), (7) and (8) (Baker 1979b):

(6) a.   The child seems to be sleepy
     b.   The child seems sleepy
(7) a.   The child appears to be sleepy
     b.   The child appears sleepy
(8) a.   The child happens to be sleepy
     b.   *The child happens sleepy

If the child learning English takes input like (6) and (7) to indicate that *to be* can optionally be deleted in certain contexts, this could lead to the production of sentences like (8b). In that case, a problem arises with the kind of evidence required to acquire the correct grammar of English, where such forms are prohibited. It appears that explicit negative evidence would be required to draw to the learner's attention to the fact that sentences like (8b) are not permitted. This is precisely the kind of evidence that is not reliably available to language learners.

In order to avoid this apparent need for negative evidence, it has been proposed that the child must in some sense be a conservative learner (e.g. Baker 1979b). In other words, children are assumed to start out with the most conservative hypothesis compatible with the input. More general hypotheses are only adopted if the input data warrant it. Sentences like (8b) will not occur in the input, hence this will not be assumed to be a possible English structure, and there will be no need for negative evidence.[2]

L1 acquisition can proceed on the basis of positive evidence if children are assumed to be guided by some form of Uniqueness Principle and by some form of conservatism. The Uniqueness Principle guarantees that the

child will know when to replace one analysis with another, rather than simply adding to previous analyses, without the benefit of negative evidence.
The conservatism hypothesis guarantees that child grammars are ordered
with the less general grammars being adopted unless there is evidence to
the contrary, so that the child will not start out with overgeneral hypotheses
which need subsequently to be disconfirmed by negative evidence.

So far, I have discussed the issues of uniqueness and conservatism in a
theory-neutral way. Indeed, many different acquisition theories propose
learning principles which clearly relate to one or other of these, including
theories that do not embrace UG (e.g. Clark 1987, O'Grady 1987, Slobin
1973). Within GB theory, certain parameters whose settings generate languages in a particular relationship to each other pose a potential acquisition
problem, similar to that illustrated in (5). For this reason, a version of the
conservatism hypothesis has been proposed, formulated as the Subset Principle (Berwick 1985; Wexler and Manzini 1987), to account for how a
learner picks the correct value of a parameter in circumstances where the
input data are ambiguous.

6.2 The Subset Principle

The Subset Principle is a particular attempt to guarantee that L1 acquisition
can be achieved with positive evidence only (Berwick 1985; Manzini and
Wexler 1987; Wexler and Manzini 1987). To see how this proposal works
one must consider two or more grammars which happen to yield languages
which are in a subset/superset relation, i.e., the grammars generate the
same subset of sentences, and one of the grammars generates additional
ones. Grammars in this kind of relationship meet the *Subset Condition*, as
shown in (9):

(9)

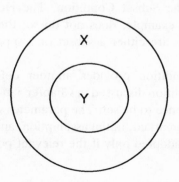

The grammar that generates the sentences X also generates the sentences Y. Y is a proper subset of X. The learnability problem is as follows: Y sentences are compatible with two grammars, the grammar that generates Y and the grammar that generates X. Suppose that the L1 learner is learning a language which only contains sentences like Y. For this language, the appropriate grammar will be the one which generates Y but not X. If, on hearing a Y sentence, the learner hypothesizes the grammar that generates X, this will result in overgeneralizations (i.e. X sentences) that cannot be disconfirmed on the basis of positive evidence. They simply do not occur in the language being learned.

The Subset Principle overcomes this learnability problem in the following way. It can be seen as an instruction to the learner: given input which could be accommodated by either of two grammars meeting the Subset Condition, the most restrictive grammar consistent with this input should be adopted. In the case of the above example, this will be the grammar that yields only Y sentences. Where the child is in fact learning a language which contains X, there will be positive evidence of X sentences which will show that the grammar yielding the subset is too restrictive. This will lead to the adoption of the grammar yielding the superset sentences X. Note that the Subset Principle is neutral about whether an acquisition stage will be found during which the child learning an X language nevertheless exercises the Y choice. Since positive evidence of X will be available, it could be that the switch to the superset grammar will occur immediately.

Different values of certain parameters of UG generate languages meeting the Subset Condition, that is, they yield languages which are in a subset/ superset relationship. Three such cases will be discussed in greater detail later in this chapter, namely the parameter of Adjacency of Case Assignment, the parameter of Configurationality, and the Governing Category Parameter. However, it is not the case that every parameter of UG yields languages meeting the Subset Condition. The Head-position Parameter (see Chapter 4), for example, does not do so; there is no way in which head-initial languages are either a subset or a superset of head-final languages.

The Subset Condition provides another definition of markedness which follows the tradition discussed in Chapter 5 in that marked values will require positive evidence to be set. The parameter setting yielding the subset language is the unmarked, initial assumption, and the value yielding the superset is marked, adopted only if the relevant positive evidence occurs.

The Subset Condition provides an independent definition of markedness, in that one can determine which value will be unmarked and which marked by calculating the possible languages that each can generate. According to this subset/superset definition of markedness, unmarked and marked phenomena will always be in a subset-superset relationship. This contrasts with the core-periphery distinction that we considered in the last chapter, where it was not always clear how markedness should be determined.

6.3 The location of markedness values

For the Subset Principle to work, the learner must somehow know which parameter setting results in the subset language. One possibility is that the markedness values of parameters are built into UG, the value of a parameter that yields a subset being defined as unmarked. In that case, the Subset Principle will be nothing more than an instruction to try the unmarked setting first, as in (10) below:[3]

(10)

Alternatively, it might be the case that the Subset Principle is sufficiently powerful to compute the possibilities each time it is faced with input, so that there is no need for markedness to be set up within UG at all (Wexler and Manzini 1987). UG would list possible parameter settings, for example, but would not list their markedness value, which would be independently computed, as in (11):

(11)

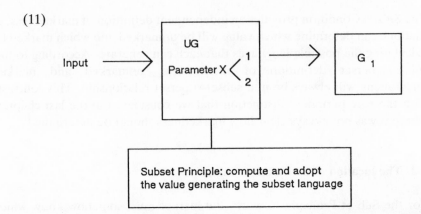

Although there are potential problems with this proposal, especially in the computational burden that seems to be involved (Fodor and Crain 1987), it has certain attractive features. It suggests that learning principles and UG may be in different 'modules' (see Chapter 7), allowing for the possibility that these modules no longer interact effectively in second language acquisition. This could explain some of the differences between L1 and L2 acquisition. In particular, it allows for the possibility that UG is still available to L2 learners but that the Subset Principle is not. In other words, L2 learners might still be constrained by the possible parameter values allowed by UG but might no longer be able to calculate the appropriate markedness values of the different settings, leading to incorrect parameter choices for the L2.

6.4   The Subset Principle and L2 acquisition

If the Subset Principle is a learning principle which helps the L1 learner to make the correct choice between different values of a parameter, the question arises as to whether it is still available in L2 acquisition. A number of possibilities come to mind, which relate to hypotheses already considered in earlier chapters:

i. The Subset Principle might operate in second language acquisition in exactly the same way that it operates in L1 acquisition, i.e., the learner adopts the parameter setting which generates the subset language unless there is evidence to the contrary. This is equivalent to the *pure UG* hypothesis that we considered in the last chapter; I will refer to it as the *subset* hypothesis for second language acquisition.

ii. In contrast to this is a position I shall call the *transfer* hypothesis, which assumes that L2 learners can no longer apply the Subset Principle directly to the L2 data; instead, they will be influenced by their L1s. Where the L1 has adopted a parameter value generating a superset language, learners will assume that this superset value is also appropriate for the L2, even if this is incorrect.

iii. Another possibility falls between these two. Some parameters of UG have more than two values meeting the Subset Condition. L2 learners might pick a value which is neither that predicted by the Subset Principle, nor that found in the L1. It would nevertheless represent a value permitted by UG, i.e., possible in natural languages.

Issues (i) and (ii) are explored by White (1989a) and Zobl (1988) and issue (iii) by Finer and Broselow (1986). The subset and transfer hypotheses make potentially opposing claims whenever one has binary parameters meeting the Subset Condition: either the unmarked subset value is chosen, or the L1 value is chosen. If the L1 value is also the subset, and the subset value shows up in second language acquisition, one cannot tell whether this is due to transfer or the operation of the Subset Principle. It is therefore important when investigating the potential operation of the Subset Principle to look at cases where the subset and transfer hypotheses make different predictions, i.e., where the L1 value generates the superset language and the L2 requires the subset.

6.4.1 *The Adjacency Condition on Case Assignment*

White (1989a) looks at a binary parameter of UG whose settings meet the Subset Condition, namely the Adjacency Condition on Case Assignment (Stowell 1981; Chomsky 1981a, 1986), which is a requirement that an NP receiving case must be next to its case assigner (1.8.2.5).

This condition explains certain facts about the distribution of English adverbs. Adverb placement is very free in English. However, adverbs cannot intervene between a verb and its direct object, since this prevents the verb from assigning case to the NP. These facts are illustrated in (12):

(12) a.   Mary slowly does her homework
     b.   Mary does her homework slowly

      c.   Slowly Mary does her homework
      d.   Mary is slowly doing her homework
      e.   *Mary does slowly her homework

Although adjacency is very strictly observed in English, this is not so in all languages. In French, for example, the equivalent of (12e) is also grammatical,[4] as can be seen in (13):

(13)   Marie fait lentement ses devoirs

The difference between (12e) and (13) suggests that the Adjacency Condition is subject to parametric variation. Chomsky (1986) proposes a parameter with values [+ strict adjacency], the English value, and [− strict adjacency], the French value.[5] These two values generate languages meeting the Subset Condition: the [− strict adjacency] option allows sentences which observe adjacency as well as sentences which violate it, whereas the [+ strict adjacency] option only allows the former. When a learner is faced with verb-object sequences in the input, the Subset Principle causes the adoption of the [+ strict adjacency] value of this parameter. The [− strict adjacency] option is only adopted on the basis of specific evidence that verb-object sequences can be interrupted, evidence such as sentences like (13) in French.

White looked at French-speaking learners of English, whose L1 grammar allows a superset of the sentences allowed in the L2, with respect to this parameter. The subset hypothesis predicts that French learners of English will pick the [+ strict adjacency] value of the parameter. This is the value which generates the subset language, and the English L2 input will not provide any evidence to suggest that the other value should be adopted. French learners of English are therefore predicted not to accept or produce sentences like (12e). In contrast, the transfer hypothesis (favoured by White) predicts that they will transfer the [− strict adjacency] value from their L1, with the consequence that forms like (12e) will be accepted and produced.

Subjects included 43 intermediate level adults, as well as adult native speakers of English to serve as controls. Tests took the form of three different tasks: a paced grammaticality judgment test, an unpaced multiple choice grammaticality judgment test, and a preference task. Sentences to be judged included grammatical English sentences observing strict adjacency and ungrammatical ones violating it. In French, both sentence types would have been grammatical.

Table 6.1   Mean scores for the paced task (White 1989a)

	− strict adjacency		+ strict adjacency	
	Controls	ESL	Controls	ESL
Totals	1.51	4.91	8.86	8.63

In the paced task, subjects read the sentences to be judged and heard them on tape at the same time. Below each sentence was a horizontal line; subjects were instructed to draw a stroke through the line to indicate the degree to which they thought the sentence was grammatical (towards the right end of the line) or ungrammatical (towards the left end of the line). The results are reported in Table 6.1. A score close to 0.5 indicates that they reject a sentence (i.e., this is accurate for the ungrammatical [− strict adjacency] sentences) and a score close to 9 indicates that they accept a sentence (i.e., it represents accuracy on the grammatical sentences). It can be seen that subjects were very accurate on the grammatical sentences, their performance not being significantly different from the control group. Subjects are noticeably less accurate on the ungrammatical sentences, which supports the claim that these ESL learners are not observing the Subset Principle in their acquisition of English, since if it were operating, it should cause the subjects to reject the adjacency violations outright.

In the multiple-choice task, subjects received a written version of the test, in which they were presented with context sentences, followed by 3 or 4 more sentences which were to be judged, as in (14). Subjects were asked to indicate whether the sentences were correct or incorrect, or whether they were not sure:

(14)   Ellen's coffee was hot.
    a.   Ellen drank slowly the hot coffee.
    b.   Slowly, Ellen drank the hot coffee.
    c.   Ellen drank the hot coffee slowly.

In Table 6.2, accuracy scores on this task are reported, i.e., correct rejection of adjacency violations and acceptance of grammatical sentences. Although subjects are very accurate on the grammatical sentences, they are significantly more likely than the controls to accept adjacency violations in English. Once again, this suggests that they are not observing the Subset Principle.

Table 6.2   Accuracy scores for the multiple choice task, in percentages (White 1989a)

	− strict adjacency		+ strict adjacency	
	Controls	*ESL*	*Controls*	*ESL*
Totals	90	57	100	90

Birdsong (1989) has raised a number of objections to the use of grammaticality judgment tasks, including the possibility that language learners adopt strategies which make it impossible to discover their underlying competence. A response bias to accept *all* sentences in a judgment task, for example, accounts for accuracy on grammatical sentences and inaccuracy on the ungrammatical ones, and could partially explain results like those in Table 6.2. In other words, this strategy, rather than transfer of the L1 parameter setting, would explain the results. However, in these tasks, subjects also had to judge ungrammatical sentences other than adjacency violations and they proved to be accurate in recognizing the ungrammaticality of these, suggesting that their performance on the adjacency violations was not simply a reflection of a bias to accept all sentences.

The third task was a preference task where subjects were not asked to accept or reject sentences but only to rate sentences against each other. Subjects had to read pairs of sentences and decide whether the first or second sentence of the pair seemed better, or whether they both seemed the same.

Test items included pairs of sentences where a sentence which observed adjacency was compared with one which violated it. Identical vocabulary and sentence structure were used in both sentences, so that the only issue to be judged was the position of the adverb. Results are presented in Table 6.3, where they are tabulated according to whether subjects preferred the sentence which maintained adjacency (+ adj), the one which violated it (− adj), or whether sentences were rated as the same.

Table 6.3   Results from the preference task, in percentages (White 1989a)

	Controls			*ESL*		
	+ adj	*− adj*	*Same*	*+ adj*	*− adj*	*Same*
Totals	97	0.5	2.5	78	1	21

The results show that the controls overwhelmingly prefer the sentences which observe strict adjacency. Only 2.5% of their responses are that the two sentences seem the same. In contrast, the ESL learners are significantly more inclined to rate the two sentences as the same: 21% of their responses are of this type. Again, this is to be expected, if the Subset Principle is not being applied to the L2 data. Adjacency violations are inconsistent with the [+ strict adjacency] value of the parameter, so if the Subset Principle were operating, it would force subjects show an invariable preference for the sentences which observe strict adjacency.

Although subjects gave significantly more responses of *same* than the control group, the majority of their responses showed a preference for the [+adj] sentences. A problem with preference tasks is that they only reveal preferences; it appears that [−adj] sentences sound better in French with some adverbs than with others. We actually need to know what these subjects would have preferred in their mother tongue, in order to determine the precise influence of the L1 parameter value in this task.

The results from these tasks support the claim that the Subset Principle does not operate in second language acquisition. Since the L2 English requires the subset [+ strict adjacency] value of the parameter, the acceptance of sentences like (12e) which are only consistent with the [− strict adjacency] value suggests, rather, that the L1 value of the parameter was transferred. If we reconsider these results in terms of markedness, the [+ strict adjacency] value is unmarked and the [− strict adjacency] is marked. What we have seen, then, is that L2 learners do not revert to the unmarked parameter setting in this case.

6.4.2 *The Configurationality Parameter*

The Configurationality Parameter provides another example where the Subset Principle appears not to operate in second language acquisition. Linguistic theories make a distinction between configurational and non-configurational languages. Configurational languages have a rich hierarchical structure, and word order is constrained. Non-configurational languages, on the other hand, have 'flat' structure, and word order is very free, in some cases allowing for discontinuous constituents.[6]

It has been suggested that configurationality constitutes a parameter (Hale 1983).[7] This parameter has two settings, [+ config] and [− config].[8] Free word order languages generated by the [− config] value of the parameter permit a superset of the sentences permitted in configurational languages; in other words, they allow the restricted word orders and many other orders as well. It is therefore the case that [+ config] must be the unmarked value of this parameter. If an L1 learner learning a non-configurational language mistakenly chooses the [+ config] setting, this will be disconfirmable on the basis of positive evidence in the form of sentences which could not possibly fit the hierarchical structure required by the [+ config] setting.

Zobl (1988) looks at the operation of the Subset Principle in second language acquisition with respect to the Configurationality Parameter. Japanese is considered by some researchers (e.g. Hale 1983) to be a non-configurational language, although this is disputed (e.g. Saito 1985). In non-configurational languages, the verb and its subcategorized complements do not form a VP constituent, in contrast to configurational languages like English. As a result, any material can be found between the verb and its complements. (This contrasts with configurational languages not observing strict adjacency, like the case of French discussed in the preceding section, where only certain adverbial adjuncts may intervene between verb and direct object. In non-configurational languages, there is no such restriction.)

Zobl investigates adult Japanese learners of English. These learners have an L1 with the superset value of this parameter, and an L2 that requires the subset. If L2 learners observe the Subset Principle, they should assume that English has a VP constituent, and they should not allow material to intervene between the verb and its complements.

Subjects were 38 adult Japanese learners of English in an intensive ESL programme at the University of Hawaii, in levels ranging from low intermediate to advanced. They were given eight English sentences with different verbs taking the following subcategorized complements: direct objects, prepositional phrases, double objects, sentential complements. Each sentence included a bracketed word or phrase at the end, and subjects were asked to mark the 'best position' in the sentence for this constituent. Zobl refers to this as a judgment task, but it is more like a preference task, since the best position is not necessarily the only position. Indeed, a problem with this study is that there was no native speaker control group, so that the judgment as to which position is 'best' is the experimenter's alone. Examples of a test sentence and the responses to it are given in (15):

(15) The girl cut her birthday cake   (with a knife)
    a.   The girl cut with a knife her birthday cake
    b.   The girl cut her birthday cake with a knife

In 36% of responses, the constituent was placed so that it interrupted the VP, as in (15a). This response was predominantly given by learners at the lower levels of proficiency, whereas the more advanced subjects inserted the detached constituent into a position which did not break up the VP, as in (15b). Zobl suggests that the less advanced learners did not in fact consider English to have a VP node and were treating English as if it were [− config], which would not be possible if the Subset Principle were operating. The more advanced learners behaved in ways which suggested that they did realize that English is [+ config]. However, the degree to which the verb and subcategorized constituents must stay together varies considerably in English. In some cases the verb and its complements must obligatorily stay together, as in (15), whereas in other cases this is optional. Sentential complements are often extraposed out of the VP. It is not clear that non-configurational responses in the optional or sentential complement cases should be counted as evidence of a non-configurational analysis of English. If these are excluded, 29% of responses suggest that English is being treated as [− config]. These results must be seen as extremely tentative, given that there were so few test sentences, in most cases only one test sentence for each kind of subcategorized complement. This is undesirable, since judgments may be influenced by the particular lexical items chosen in a test sentence and may not generalize to other sentences with the same structure.

Zobl's results, if replicated, suggest once again that L2 learners do not initially revert to the unmarked parameter setting. In this case, the initial assumption of Japanese learners of English was that the L2 is [− config], like the L1. However, the more advanced subjects appeared to have changed from the superset [− config] value to the subset [+ config] value, as required by English. Zobl suggests that there are other properties of configurational languages which more advanced learners become aware of from positive evidence, which are incompatible with the [− config] setting and which lead them to reset this parameter.[9]

Zobl's study brings to mind a further issue which is of considerable potential interest, namely the fact that some parameters are nested. In certain cases, a parameter setting will feed into another, i.e., be a necessary precursor for another. One of the constraints on word order in configurational languages is the Adjacency Condition on Case Assignment, which is itself subject to parametric variation, as we have seen (6.4.1). Thus, these two parameters (Configurationality and Adjacency) are in the kind of relationship shown in (16):

(16)

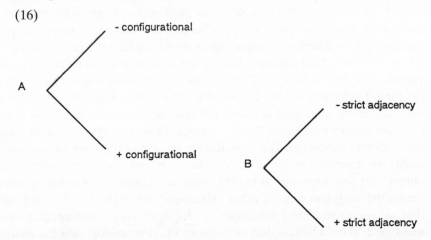

- configurational

A

+ configurational

B

- strict adjacency

+ strict adjacency

If a language is non-configurational, Adjacency is irrelevant because there is no VP constituent and NPs do not get case from verbs. In configurational languages, on the other hand, the question of ordering of verb and object in a structural configuration is crucial, and the Adjacency Parameter becomes relevant, dictating that the adjacency requirement can only be relaxed in certain rather limited respects. Japanese learners of English, then, presumably have to do two things: they must set the Configurationality Parameter and then they must set the Adjacency Parameter, i.e., having worked out that English is configurational, they must also work out how strict the adjacency requirement is.

Zobl only considers the Configurationality Parameter, not the Adjacency Parameter, but it would be interesting to tease out whether the advanced learners, who had reset to the [+ config] value of the Configurationality Parameter, had also set to the [+ strict adjacency] value of the Adjacency Parameter. It is conceivable that L2 learners will end up making interconnecting choices that represent neither the L1 nor the L2 but are permissible in natural languages; for example, if Japanese learners chose [+ config], [− strict adjacency], their interlanguage would constitute a possible natural language (like French) but one which is exemplified in neither the L1 nor the L2.[10]

6.4.3 *The Governing Category Parameter*

The third parameter that has been investigated by second language acquisition researchers interested in the Subset Principle is the Governing Category Parameter of Wexler and Manzini (1987). This parameter is of particular interest because it has five values rather than two, which means that there are other values in addition to those found in the L1 and the L2, so that the transfer and subset hypotheses do not represent the only possibilities.

This parameter relates to the Binding Theory, specifically the locality domain in which different kinds of pronouns must be bound or free. Here, we shall only consider reflexive pronouns (himself, herself, etc). These fall under Principle A of the Binding Theory, which states that an anaphor must be bound in its governing category (1.8.2.7). Languages vary as to what counts as a governing category. Wexler and Manzini (1987) propose that there are five different governing categories and that this is best accounted for by a Governing Category Parameter (GCP) with five values. In the discussion here, I shall reduce these to three values, for ease of exposition. In addition, I shall oversimply them, in order not to get too technical.

Languages like English exemplify one of the values of the GCP. In English, a reflexive must be bound within the same clause, regardless of whether this is finite or non-finite, as can be seen in (17):

(17) a. $John_j$ washed $himself_j$
     b. $John_j$ said [that $Fred_f$ washed $himself_{f/*j}$]
     c. $John_j$ wanted [$Fred_f$ to wash $himself_{f/*j}$]
     d. $Keith_k$ said [that $John_j$ said [that $Fred_f$ washed $himself_{f/*j/*k}$]]

In (17b) and (17c), *himself* takes *Fred* as its antecedent but not *John*, since *John* is not in the same clause as the reflexive. In (17d), neither *Keith* nor *John* can serve as antecedent, for the same reason.

In some languages, antecedents for reflexives are not limited to the nearest clause. A number of languages treat reflexives differently depending on whether they occur in finite or nonfinite clauses; in Russian, for example, the governing category must be finite. Sentences like (17b) and (17d) will behave as English does: where the embedded clause is finite, it is the governing category. In the equivalents of (17c), however, either *Fred* or *John* may be the antecedent of the reflexive, since only the main clause is finite.

Other languages allow an even wider range of antecedents. In Korean and Japanese, the governing category is the main clause. This means that in the equivalents of (17b) and (17c), either *Fred* or *John* may be the antecedent of the reflexive, and in (17d), *Keith* or *Fred* or *John* can serve as antecedent.

In all cases, the anaphor may be bound in the governing category or within a lesser category that falls inside the governing category. For example, as described above, an anaphor in Korean can be bound in the main clause or in any clause embedded in the sentence. Thus we have the relevant subset/superset relationships for the GCP, as illustrated in (18):

(18)

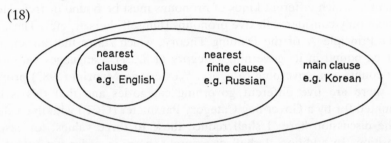

The values of the GCP form a hierarchy. Languages like English, where the tightest locality restriction on antecedents is found, represent the subset value of the GCP. Languages like Korean and Japanese represent the largest superset. Languages like Russian are a superset of English but a subset of Korean and Japanese.

Recently, a number of researchers have begun to investigate the GCP in L2 acquisition. If the Subset Principle still operates, learners should assume that the L2 only allows very local antecedents, i.e., that the nearest clause is the governing category.

Finer and Broselow (1986) report on a pilot study on the L2 acquisition of English reflexives by adult Koreans. Here the L1 exemplifies the widest superset value and the L2 the subset. They outline four possibilities for L2 acquisition in this context:

i.   The superset L1 value is transferred to the L2
ii. The subset L2 value is adopted immediately
iii. An intermediate value is adopted
iv. An 'unnatural' possibility is adopted[11]

Possibilities (i) and (ii) represent the transfer and subset hypotheses that were considered above with respect to the Adjacency Parameter. (iii) represents an interesting possibility that simply does not arise in the case of binary parameters.

Finer and Broselow tested six Korean-speaking adults who were learning English in the USA, five intermediate level and one advanced. The task was picture identification. Subjects were shown pairs of pictures with two easily identifiable characters (Mr. Fat and Mr. Thin) who were imagining things in cartoon-style bubbles. Subjects heard sentences such as (19) and (20):

(19) Mr. Fat thinks that Mr. Thin will paint himself
(20) Mr. Thin asks Mr. Fat to paint himself

They were asked to point to the picture they thought most appropriate for the sentence they had heard or to indicate if both pictures could represent the sentence. (Sentences like (19) and (20) would be ambiguous in Korean.) There were 16 test sentences, half containing reflexives. Half of the sentences contained finite embedded clauses like (19) and half nonfinite clauses like (20).

Results on the eight sentences containing reflexives are given in Table 6.4. Responses to the finite embedded clauses strongly favoured a local antecedent, in contrast to the nonfinite embedded clauses, where nonlocal responses were also quite frequent. If one only considers the former results, learners appear to be observing the Subset Principle rather than transferring the L1 value of the parameter. Transfer of the L1 value would predict a far higher incidence of nonlocal antecedents, as well as results indicating that either NP could serve as the antecedent. However, the results from the nonfinite sentences are inconsistent with the operation of the Subset Principle; although the majority of responses are still local, there are many more nonlocal responses where they choose the matrix subject as the antecedent of the reflexive.

Table 6.4 Results from sentences containing reflexives, in percentages (Finer and Broselow 1986)

	Local antecedent	Nonlocal	Either
Finite	92	8	0
Nonfinite	58	38	4

This differential treatment of finite and nonfinite clauses does not stem from the Subset Principle. It also does not stem from Korean. Neither English nor Korean, though at opposite ends of the governing category hierarchy, distinguishes between finite and nonfinite clauses with regard to reflexives. In fact, as Finer and Broselow note, Korean does not have an overt finite/nonfinite distinction. English requires the minimal clause as the governing category, regardless of whether it is finite. However, languages in the middle of the governing category hierarchy distinguish between finite and nonfinite clauses as far as governing categories for reflexives are concerned; that is, reflexives must be locally bound in tensed clauses but need not be in tenseless ones. This is what the Korean learners of English seem to be doing; they have picked a value of the parameter allowed in natural languages but it is the value of neither the L1 nor the L2, suggesting that they are driven exclusively by neither the Subset Principle nor transfer.[12]

One might argue that these results can be dismissed as being from a very small pilot study. However, this study has inspired several others, which look at the same or related issues with much larger numbers of subjects. Finer (1989) tested 30 Korean-speaking and 14 Japanese-speaking learners of English in the USA on the same kinds of structures, including 22 sentences like (19) and (20). Again, a picture identification task was used, but this time subjects had to choose out of four pictures rather than two. The results are presented in Table 6.5.

Table 6.5   Results from sentences containing reflexives, in percentages (Finer 1989)

	Local antecedent	Nonlocal	Other
Koreans			
Finite	97	2	1
Nonfinite	88	7	5
Japanese			
Finite	91	5	3
Nonfinite	76	12	12

The differences in choice of local antecedents in the two clause types are significant. As before, responses to the finite embedded clauses give local antecedents almost exclusively, which is not the case for the infinitival clauses. The incidence of nonlocal responses is inconsistent with the Subset Principle. In addition, subjects were tested in their mother tongue. There was a strong preference for nonlocal antecedents in both Korean and Japanese, suggesting that transfer of the L1 value does not account for the L2 learners' behaviour. Again, these results suggest that the subjects may have adopted a value of the GCP which is that of neither the L1 nor the L2.

Two other studies have reported results similar to those of Finer and Broselow, although with some interesting differences. Hirakawa (1989) looks at the GCP with Japanese learners of English. Her subjects were at high school in Japan; in other words, it was foreign language learning in the classroom. 65 Japanese-speakers in Grades 10, 11, 12 and 13 (ages 15 to 19 years) were presented with 25 sentences containing at least two noun-phrases and a reflexive pronoun. Potential antecedents were listed under each sentence, and subjects were asked to circle the antecedent for the reflexive. Results from the sentences equivalent to those used by Finer and Broselow are given in Table 6.6.[13]

As in the case of Finer's (1989) study, the difference between the finite and nonfinite choices of nonlocal antecedents is significant. However, there is a much higher incidence of nonlocal responses for the finite clauses than Finer found. This is not consistent with the intermediate value of the parameter which **requires** local antecedents in finite clauses. One possible explanation is that Hirakawa's subjects were, in fact, transferring their L1 value of the GCP. As they were probably less advanced in their English than those studied by Finer and Broselow (1986), Finer (1989), it is possible that these results represent an earlier stage of L2 acquisition. However, if this is the correct interpretation, it is still clear that they are not treating English exactly like Japanese. A Japanese-speaking control group took a Japanese version of the test, and nonlocal responses predominate, even

Table 6.6   Results from sentences containing reflexives, in percentages (Hirakawa 1989)

	Local antecedent	Nonlocal	Either
Finite	77	17	6
Nonfinite	54	37	8

though local antecedents are permitted in Japanese. In contrast, the predominant response of the learners of English is to choose a local antecedent.

A third study reports results similar to Hirakawa's, namely the choice of nonlocal antecedents even in finite clauses. Thomas (1989) looked at whether native speakers of Spanish (n=29) and Chinese (n=24) would assume that reflexives in English must have antecedents within the same clause. She assumes that Spanish is like English with respect to the GC parameter, allowing only antecedents in the same clause, and that Chinese is like Korean and Japanese, allowing nonlocal antecedents. The task was similar to that used by Hirakawa but all sentences contained finite embedded clauses (i.e. the finite/nonfinite distinction was not studied). Six of these sentences were equivalent to those studied in the experiments reported above.[14] Results from these sentences are given in Table 6.7.

Table 6.7   Results from finite sentences containing reflexives, in percentages (Thomas 1989).

	Local antecedent	Nonlocal	Either
Spanish	60	19	21
Chinese	69	7	24

Once again, it is clear that the Subset Principle cannot be operating. The nonlocal responses, as well as those indicating that either a nonlocal or a local NP can be the antecedent, are inconsistent with the subset value of the GCP. The results from the Chinese-speakers could be explained in terms of the transfer of the L1 value but this is not possible for the Spanish. Even though their L1 requires the subset value of the parameter, this is not the value they adopt in the L2, suggesting once again that the L1 does not play a major role here. However, the value that these subjects adopt cannot be the intermediate value that Finer and Broselow suggest, since the intermediate value requires local antecedents in finite clauses.

6.4.4   *The Governing Category Parameter: summary*

The four studies that look at the operation of the Governing Category Parameter in L2 acquisition report results which are inconsistent with the operation of the Subset Principle. If the Subset Principle were operating in L2 acquisition, learners of English should correctly limit their choice of an antecedent of a reflexive to a nounphrase within the same clause. Native-speakers of Korean, Japanese, Chinese and Spanish, of different ages and learning English in different circumstances, all fail to do this. They are unable to revert to the unmarked parameter setting in this case, as was also reported by the studies on the Adjacency and Configurationality Parameters.

The results from these studies also suggest that the behaviour of these learners cannot be attributed solely to the operation of transfer. Thomas's Spanish-speaking subjects do not treat English like Spanish, and Finer and Broselow's Korean-speaking and Japanese-speaking subjects do not treat English like Korean or Japanese.

What is not so clear is what value of the GCP L2 learners initially adopt. Finer and Broselow propose that their subjects adopt one of the intermediate values of the parameter, but the results of the other studies suggest that the widest superset value is being adopted. Possibly these differences are due to differences in the level of English attained by subjects in the different studies; longitudinal or cross-sectional studies would help to resolve this point.

Another question of considerable interest is whether L2 learners are eventually able to achieve the value of the GCP required by English. Thomas (1989) included a group of four very advanced learners of English; their responses were identical to those of a native-speaker control group. That is, their responses were almost exclusively in favour of the local antecedent. Hirakawa (1989) gives a breakdown of responses by individual subjects, and ten of them give only local responses to all 25 test sentences, whether finite or nonfinite, just like her English-speaking control group. An additional six subjects made only one non-local choice in the test as a whole. These results suggest that even if learners pick the wrong value of the GCP during the course of acquisition, some of them are able to attain the correct L2 value.

6.5 Failure of the Subset Principle and accessibility of UG

Principles and parameters of UG severely constrain the range of learners' hypotheses; the Subset Principle is a learning principle which constrains the order in which hypotheses are entertained. The research reported in 6.4 suggests that the Subset Principle does not operate effectively in second language acquisition, that L2 learners do not start out with the most restricted parameter setting compatible with the L2 data but adopt settings with overgeneral consequences, in some cases based on the L1. This failure of the Subset Principle does **not** imply that UG is inaccessible in second language acquisition. In all the cases discussed above, the L2 learners adopted a parameter value permitted by UG, although not the value required by the L2.

It is important to understand that the ability to switch from the L1 value of a parameter to some other value shows that UG must still be operating, as does the initial adoption of any non-L1 value of a parameter. The parameter values are part of UG. If UG is inaccessible and L2 learners construct grammars only by general problem-solving, there is no reason why they should not adopt logical possibilities which do not represent parameters of UG; there is nothing in the L2 data alone which dictates that only a specified set of possibilities is allowed. If L2 learners have no access to UG at all, or only via their L1, then we do not expect them to arrive at other values of parameters, either L2 values or values which are neither L1 nor L2.

If anything, the results reported in this chapter suggest that it is the Subset Principle which is no longer available to L2 learners, rather than UG itself. That is, looking back at the diagram in (11), UG and the parameter values are still available, but the ability to compute which value leads to the subset language is lost. In other words, even though the learning principle is no longer available, UG is: the types of hypotheses entertained by learners who were not observing the Subset Principle were nevertheless within the range permitted by UG. Thus, with respect to the interaction of UG and learning principles, L1 and L2 acquisition would be alike in that they are limited by the same constraints but different in that they do not try out the various possibilities in the same order. It would be of considerable interest to investigate whether other learning principles, such as the Uniqueness Principle, are also inaccessible to L2 learners. See Rutherford (1988) for some interesting speculation on this question.

The failure of the Subset Principle offers a potential explanation of the results reported in Chapter 5, where unmarked structures did not prevail in the IL to the extent predicted by various researchers. Many of the structures studied in the markedness framework in fact meet the Subset Condition. For example, a language allowing both preposition stranding and piedpiping is a superset of one allowing only piedpiping; a language allowing both double object and NP PP complements is a superset of one allowing only NP PP complements; a language allowing both lexical and empty complementizers is a superset of one allowing only lexical complementizers. If the Subset Principle is unable to operate, this would explain why marked structures were not excluded from the interlanguages of subjects in the various studies described earlier.

6.6 Resetting parameters: the nature of the triggering evidence

In this section, we return to the situations outlined in 6.1, this time considering them in the context of parameter values and second language acquisition. Even if the Subset Principle does not operate, this does not necessarily mean that L2 learners are permanently committed to inappropriate grammars for the L2. That is, evidence can lead to grammar change in L2 acquisition, just as it does in L1, although different kinds of evidence may be needed to bring this about.

6.6.1 *Subsets to supersets*

Where the input is consistent with two parameter values meeting the Subset Condition, L1 learners start off with the value which generates the narrower range of structures (6.2). If they hear input which does not fall within this range, the value generating the superset language is motivated. In this way, the change from one grammar to another is brought about by positive evidence.

In principle, such change could take place in second language acquisition even if the Subset Principle no longer functions as a learning principle. There will still be circumstances where the L2 learner initially adopts a grammar which is a subset of that required by the L2; for example, if the mother tongue represents the subset value and this value is transferred in circumstances where the L2 in fact represents the superset, the L2 learner may indeed start out with a subset hypothesis, but not because of the Subset Principle, as shown in (21):

(21)

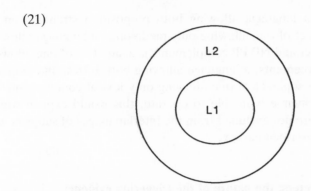

In such cases, there will be positive data from the L2 indicating a need for change to a more inclusive grammar. In principle, at least, the L2 learner might notice immediately that the L2 input is not consistent with the L1 value.

Do L2 learners in fact take note of positive L2 evidence when it is available like this? White (1989a and to appear) administered French versions of the tasks relevant to the Adjacency Parameter (i.e., the paced judgment task, the multiple choice judgment task and a different version of the preference task) to various groups of English-speaking learners of French, in Grades 5 (average age 11) and 6 (average age 12). In all three tasks, she found that learners of French were significantly less likely than native speakers to accept adjacency violations in the judgment tasks or to rate them as *same* in the preference task. However, adjacency violations were not overwhelmingly rejected either, suggesting that these learners were not sticking completely to the subset L1 value of the parameter. In other words, they were taking the positive evidence from French into account, but only partially.

6.6.2 *Value X to Value Y*

Some cases of parameter resetting will fit figure (4), where one value has to be replaced by another and the Subset Condition is not met. Here any failure of the Subset Principle in L2 acquisition is simply irrelevant. In such cases, again, positive evidence in the L2 should be available to motivate a resetting. For example, the parameter of Head-position is a binary parameter with two values, head-initial or head-final. Japanese learners of English have the L1 with head-final and the L2 with head-initial. The positive input from English will give clear evidence of the head-initial nature of English (e.g. verb object word order, prepositions rather than postpositions, relative clauses following head nouns, etc), so that this parameter should be set or reset without much difficulty. (In principle, the learner might start off with the L1 value but notice immediately that there is positive evidence to disconfirm this.) The same applies the other way around (i.e. English L1, Japanese L2). Evidence suggests that the L2 value of the parameter is acquired early and without difficulty (Rutherford 1983).[15] It is important to note that this situation is not limited to binary parameters: one might have a multi-valued parameter whose values do not meet the Subset Condition. If so, it should be possible to change from any one value to any other with positive evidence only.[16]

6.6.3 *Supersets to subsets*

In cases where the L2 learner mistakenly adopts a value leading to language which is a superset of the actual L2, the question of what kind of evidence motivates parameter resetting is trickier. If the L2 learner has not adopted the most conservative analysis compatible with the L2 input, interlanguage forms will include overgeneralizations of various kinds, and certain misinterpretations of L2 input are likely to occur. For example, the French-speaking learner of English will produce forms like (22) and the Japanese-speaking learner of English may interpret (23) incorrectly:

(22)   John drinks slowly his coffee
(23)   Mary thinks that Jane hates herself

There appears to be no positive L2 input that sentences like (22) are ungrammatical. They are nonoccurring in English, but nonoccurrence does not guarantee ungrammaticality; there are many other sentences that a learner will not hear which are nevertheless grammatical. Furthermore, this presupposes that learners are able to notice nonoccurrence which is not at all obviously the case (nor is it clear that native speakers can do this). It is also not clear what positive input will indicate to the learner that an interpretation of (23) where *Mary* is the antecedent of *herself* is excluded in English. Presumably context will indicate on particular occasions that the interpretation must be that *Jane* is the antecedent, but finding out that the local NP is the antecedent in certain circumstances is not the same thing as finding out that the nonlocal NP may never be the antecedent.

The assumption in L1 acquisition is that learners never make such problematical overgeneralizations because they are constrained by the Subset Principle. We have already seen that the Subset Principle does not appear to operate effectively in L2 acquisition. This means that negative evidence may be required to lead to resetting from the superset to the subset value of a parameter (or in any cases where the L2 learner's interlanguage is a superset of the L2). In other words, it may be necessary to make it explicit to the L2 learner, via grammar teaching, error correction, or other forms of consciousness raising (Rutherford 1987), that certain sentence types are ungrammatical in the L2, or that certain interpretations are possible and others impossible. For example, one may need to instruct French-speaking learners of English that (22) is ungrammatical, and Japanese-speaking learners of English may need to be instructed that there is only one possible interpretation of (23). This is not a case of instructing learners as to principles of UG, which is surely unlikely to be effective. But given that parameters of UG allow a variety of languages, and that learners may pick the 'wrong', superset value in some cases, negative evidence may be the only alternative since positive evidence is in principle unavailable.

Although L2 learners get themselves into situations where negative evidence appears to be necessary, it is still an open question as to whether they can make effective use of such evidence, whether it can serve as an alternative form of input to the ILG in circumstances where no positive evidence is available.[17] This is an area where controlled research would be useful.[18]

In some cases, resetting may never take place at all, presumably either because of the absence of the relevant kind of input, or because L2 learners are not able to make use of it even if it occurs. Failure to reset parameters, then, will lead to fossilization, to the use of superset structures when the subset is actually required. In other cases, resetting does happen; a number of the studies considered in earlier sections have pointed out that more advanced learners no longer inappropriately adopt superset hypotheses for the L2. We do not, however, know how this was achieved, whether by negative evidence or by subtle positive evidence which only becomes available at later stages of acquisition, as suggested by Zobl (1988).

6.6.4 *Directionality revisited*

In 5.6, certain directional predictions concerning parameter resetting were discussed, with respect to the Prodrop Parameter. Phinney (1987) argued that it is easier to reset from the marked value of a parameter to the unmarked, whereas White (1986b, 1988b) argued the opposite. Rephrasing this discussion in terms of parameter values and the Subset Condition, White's reasons for assuming that it is easier to reset from L1 unmarked to L2 marked should become clearer. If the L1 has the unmarked, subset value of a parameter and the L2 requires the marked superset, there will be positive L2 evidence to disconfirm the L1 parameter value. On the other hand, if the L1 has the superset value and the L2 requires the subset, the only kind of disconfirming evidence appears to be negative evidence. White's prediction, then, is that resetting of parameters is in principle possible but that there will be directional differences, it being easier to reset using positive evidence rather than negative.

6.7 Conclusion

In this chapter, the role of the Subset Principle in second language acquisition has been considered. Experimental evidence suggests that the Subset Principle is no longer available, causing learners to create ILGs which overgenerate in various ways. This overgeneration nevertheless represents possible parameter settings, suggesting that the L2 learner's interlanguage is still constrained by UG. In other words, it is possible that UG remains accessible to L2 learners but that they no longer have available the learning principles which allow L1 learners to access parameter values in a particular order.

6.8 Further reading

i.   For technical details on the Subset Principle in L1 acquisition — *Berwick* 1985, *Manzini and Wexler* 1987, *Wexler and Manzini* 1987.
ii.   For the Governing Category Parameter and another related parameter — *Manzini and Wexler* 1987, *Wexler and Manzini* 1987.
iii.   For discussion of the positive and negative evidence issues in L2 acquisition — *Bley-Vroman* (1986), *Rutherford* (1987), *Schwartz* (1987), *White* (in press).

Notes to Chapter 6

1. Interestingly enough, cases of negative evidence that have recently been discussed in the L1 acquisition literature (e.g. Hirsh-Pasek et al. 1984, Bohannon and Stanowicz 1988) involve the parent rephrasing a child's incorrect form. In other words, the parent provides a positive example of the correct alternative, and does not indicate that the child's form is incorrect. This would appear to be positive evidence, not negative, and presupposes something like uniqueness.

2. A problem is that children do, of course, make generalizations that go beyond input, so that the conservatism thesis has to be sufficiently refined to allow certain kinds of generalization and exclude others. See Bowerman (1987), Pinker (1984) for discussion.

3. However, this means that it need not really be a subset principle, i.e., any principle which says *pick unmarked first* will work provided markedness is defined.

4. Sentences like (12a), where the adverb is between the subject and the verb, are ungrammatical in French.

5. More recently, it has been suggested that the differences between English and French with respect to adverb placement fall out from a parameter involving the possibility of verb raising in French but not English (Pollock 1989).

6. For example, a nounphrase can be broken up so that the determiner and noun are not found together, but are separated by something like the verb, which is not a constituent of the nounphrase.

7. However, there is considerable disagreement about this. Many linguists argue that all languages are basically configurational.

8. According to Hale, the crucial distinction between the two settings relates to the operation of the Projection Principle (1.8.2.3).

9. This discussion is rather technical and relates to properties of the English passive and how it would be parsed.

10. Indeed, the possibility of interlocking parameters is independent of the Subset Principle issue; parameters which do not meet the Subset Condition may nevertheless have other parameters dependent on them.

11. For example, a requirement that the antecedent must exclusively be in the main clause, or exclusively in a non-finite clause, etc.

12. One thing militates against this analysis. There should have been more responses indicating ambiguity (i.e. more choices of *either*). However, a number of researchers have found that native speakers and language learners given ambiguous sentences only notice one of the interpretations.

13. In addition, Hirakawa included sentences with two embedded clauses. I will not discuss these results here, but they also show a difference between finite and nonfinite clauses with respect to locality of antecedents.

14. Other issues to do with reflexive interpretation were also investigated and will not be reported on here.

15. Difficulties with this parameter that were discussed in Chapter 4, relate either to complex

sentences (Flynn 1987b) or to German (Clahsen and Muysken 1986), which is not a clear-cut case.

16.   In other words, it is presumably accidental that the only multi-valued parameter that has been investigated in the second language acquisition context is one which meets the Subset Condition.

17.   Schwartz (1987) argues that negative evidence cannot be used by L2 learners.

18.   See White 1989c for an example.

7 | Universal Grammar and second language acquisition

7.1 Partial access to UG?

Research discussed in earlier chapters has not provided an unequivocal answer about the role of UG in L2 acquisition. Some L2 learners clearly do attain complex and subtle knowledge which does not derive solely from the L1; this is unexplained if L2 learning proceeds only by means of problem-solving and hypothesis-testing, and suggests that UG must be involved. For example, some of the experimental research discussed in Chapter 3 supports the claim that fixed principles of UG which are not instantiated in the L1 are nevertheless acquired in L2 acquisition. Where principles of UG are parameterized, as discussed in Chapters 4 and 6, some L2 learners are capable of acquiring a parameter setting which is different from that operating in the L1.

These are successes but there are failures as well. Some of the research we have considered suggests that learners fail to acquire principles not instantiated in the L1, and fail to reset parameters to the L2 value, both problematic for the assumption that UG is actively available. Markedness (however defined) does not appear to interact with UG in the same fashion as it does in L1 acquisition.

In Chapter 2, it was suggested that theories of L2 acquisition must not only account for successful L2 acquisition but also be responsive to differences between L1 and L2 acquisition. We have seen that one way of explaining L1/L2 differences has been to assume that UG is totally unavailable (Clahsen and Muysken 1986; Schachter 1988b). Since much of the research discussed in this book has demonstrated that L2 learners possess the kind of complex and subtle knowledge that derives from UG, this explanation is not a satisfactory one. We appear to have a paradox: on the one hand, UG must be available to explain why L2 learners show UG effects in their ILGs; on the other hand, UG appears not to be available, since by no means all L2 learners access new principles and parameters required by the L2.

How can this paradox be resolved? Returning to the various hypotheses for UG in L2 acquisition that have been investigated throughout this book, it seems uncontroversial that the pure UG hypothesis (i.e., the claim of total equivalence of UG in L1 and L2 acquisition) is not supported. It also now appears to be generally agreed that UG is not totally inaccessible, that L2 learners do exhibit language behaviour which must have originated in UG. Compare, for example, the assumptions made in the papers by Clahsen and Muysken (1986) and Clahsen and Muysken (1989). In the former paper, UG is argued to be totally unavailable; in the latter paper, it is suggested that fixed principles but not parameters are available. Similarly, Schachter (1988b) assumes no access, whereas Schachter (1988a) assumes UG to be accessible but only via the L1, a position also held by Bley-Vroman (1989). Thus, a consensus appears to be developing that there is partial access to UG in L2 acquisition. However, although the insight that access is only partial may well be correct, it is not at all clear that this is because UG can only be accessed via the L1: much of the research discussed in this book has demonstrated that L2 learners exhibit complex and subtle knowledge which is not L1-based. Thus a major future research goal for this field should be to try to specify precisely the conditions under which UG is accessible, and what factors inhibit the operation of UG in L2 acquisition.

In fact, much of the research discussed in this book already provides partial answers to these questions. In this chapter, we shall reconsider some of the differences between L1 and L2 acquisition outlined in Chapter 2, and discuss how they can be accommodated within theories that assume accessibility of UG. In addition, it will be suggested that differences between L1 and L2 acquisition, and the difficulties of L2 learners, can in part be attributed to differences in the way UG interacts with other cognitive domains in non-primary acquisition.

7.2 L1 and L2 acquisition differences revisited

7.2.1 *Degree of success*

One of the differences between L1 and L2 acquisition that is often advanced as problematic for the UG hypothesis is the fact that L1 learners almost invariably attain a grammar which is indistinguishable from other native speakers, in contrast to L2 learners (Bley-Vroman 1989; Schachter 1988b). We can now reconsider this issue in the UG context. It is not sufficient to point to error-ridden second language performance and argue that this is evidence against the operation of UG. One must distinguish between principles and parameters of UG, on the one hand, and language-specific properties of the L2, on the other. While it is true that L2 learners often have considerable difficulties in acquiring language-specific properties of the L2, this is not necessarily a reflection of the non-operation of UG. As for the principles and parameters of UG that have so far been investigated, much of the research suggests that L2 learners are constrained by UG. They do not produce forms that constitute violations of principles of UG, nor interpret utterances in ways inconsistent with principles of UG. In other words, the ILG of the L2 learner is a *possible grammar*, where a possible grammar is one that falls within the range permitted by UG, even though it often is not equivalent to the actual grammar internalized by native speakers.

7.2.2 *Mother tongue*

Another difference between L1 and L2 acquisition that was raised in Chapter 2 was the fact that L2 learners necessarily know at least one language other than the language being acquired. We have seen how the theory of parameters in fact allows mother tongue knowledge to be accommodated within a theory of L2 acquisition. Both the UG hypothesis and the UG-is-dead hypothesis assume that parameter theory offers an account of language transfer; they differ as to whether they consider the L1 to provide the learner's only access to UG, or whether L1 parameter settings are simply an interim assumption of the L2 learner before resetting takes place.

7.2.3 *Fossilization*

Fossilization (that is, getting 'stuck' at a point short of the L2 grammar) is something that happens in L2 acquisition but not L1. In fact, some kinds of fossilization may be a direct consequence of the failure of the Subset Principle. In Chapter 6, it was suggested that learning principles are distinct from UG and that the Subset Principle no longer operates in L2 acquisition. In consequence, the L2 learner does not necessarily start out by adopting the grammar which generates the subset language. When learners adopt parameter settings which generate a superset of the language actually permitted by the L2, their grammars are likely candidates for fossilization, since there will be no positive evidence to lead to parameter resetting in these circumstances. Some forms of obvious fossilization, then, would be the result of carrying over a superset grammar from the L1, failing to apply the Subset Principle to the L2 data (White 1989a). Failure to reset to the L2 parameter value is a particular case of this form of fossilization.

7.2.4 *Input*

This same failure of the Subset Principle can also account for another difference between L1 and L2 acquisition, namely the effectiveness of instruction and correction. It is standardly assumed that explicit instruction and negative evidence are not effective when they are available in L1 acquisition (1.4.3), whereas they are assumed to be effective in second language acquisition, although there is considerable disagreement as to what methods of instruction are most beneficial, and the extent to which grammar teaching and correction are useful. The operation of the Subset Principle in L1 acquisition prevents learners from adopting overgeneral grammars, so that learning is able to proceed on the basis of positive evidence only. However, due to the failure of the Subset Principle, L2 learners do get themselves into situations where naturalistic positive evidence does not suffice to disconfirm incorrect hypotheses. One of the reasons, then, why instruction and correction may be more effective in second language acquisition is that there is in fact no possible alternative; in L1 acquisition negative evidence is superfluous (because positive evidence will suffice) but in L2 acquisition it is not (White 1987a, in press).

7.2.5 *Age*

Most of the research on the role of UG in L2 acquisition has not been able to control for the age factor in an effective manner. Many supposedly adult learners in fact started L2 acquisition at the ages of 11, 12 or 13. It may be that all that has been demonstrated so far is that UG is involved in child and adolescent L2 acquisition, and that the issue of adult L2 acquisition is still open. However, assuming that the kinds of successes and failures that have been demonstrated for UG in L2 acquisition hold true for adult learners in general, a possibility is that some adult problems stem not from the non-operation of UG but from the way it interacts with other cognitive domains.

7.3 Modularity

7.3.1 *The language module*

A number of current theories of human cognition recognize different cognitive modules, although there is considerable disagreement as to what aspects of cognition are modular, to what extent modules are independent of one another and how they interact (Fodor 1983; papers in Garfield 1987). Proponents of modularity argue for distinct domains for various computational aspects of perception and language, which function more or less autonomously and which are relatively impervious to information from outside. A basic assumption of the theory of grammar that we have been assuming is that there is a language module. The autonomous language module processes linguistic input and the output of this processing is passed on to central processors, which are not domain specific and which bring together information from various areas, such as memory, real-world knowledge, and beliefs. Even within the language module, there appear to be different sub-domains. Universal grammar, the language-specific grammar, the language parser, the language learning principles, might reasonably be considered as partially independent from one another but interacting in certain ways. These various possibilities are diagrammed in Figure 7.1.

It is possible that the interaction of modules is different in L1 and L2 acquisition and that the relative lack of success of L2 learners is attributable to changes in modular interaction, or in the interaction of the sub-components of the language module, rather than the non-operation of UG. For example, it has already been suggested that one difference between L1 and L2 acquisition concerns the availability of the Subset Principle as a learning principle. Couched in modular terms, the claim would be that there is a breakdown between two of the sub-domains that form part of the language module.

A number of researchers have recently begun to explore the implications of modular interactions for second language acquisition (Schwartz 1987; Sharwood Smith, to appear; Zobl 1989). This appears to be a fruitful line of inquiry, especially as theories develop as to the precise content of each of the cognitive modules, and they way they relate to each other and to the central processors.

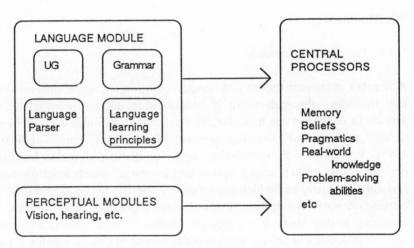

Figure 7.1 Cognitive modularity

7.3.2 *The competition model*

A proposal that fits with the idea of a breakdown in the way modules interact is the competition model of Felix (1985) who suggests that UG is still available to adult learners but that problem-solving is also utilized in constructing a grammar for the L2. This contrasts with the position of Bley-Vroman (1989) or Clahsen and Muysken (1986) who assume that problem-solving effectively replaces UG. Felix suggests that problem-solving procedures and UG compete in terms of the analyses of L2 data that they allow.

According to Fodor (1983), problem-solving belongs in the central processors because it is not domain-specific and draws on information from many different areas. To rephrase Felix's idea in terms of Fodor's distinctions, the difference between L1 and L2 acquisition would be that in L1 acquisition only the language module processes linguistic input but in L2 acquisition both the language module and the central processors try to analyze input. This results in competition because the language module and the central processors work in very different ways from each other, the language module being rapid, automatic, and unconscious, while the central processors are conscious and slower. This dual way of dealing with L2 input leads L2 learners to learn less effectively than L1. For a related idea, see Schwartz (1986) who argues that Krashen's (1981) acquisition/learning distinction stems from this dichotomy: acquisition results from the language module, learning from the central processors.

Felix suggests that his proposal can account for age effects in second language acquisition, on the assumption that the emergence of problem-solving abilities is linked to puberty, which is often claimed to mark the end of a critical period for language acquisition. He can also account for the presence of UG-driven language behaviour in adult learners, since UG is assumed still to be in operation. There is something intuitively appealing about this hypothesis of competition between the language module and the central processors. However, a detailed theory is required of precisely how problem-solving works, in order to make specific predictions as to what the competition will consist of, and why there is competition; after all, another logical possibility is the two would conspire to make adults better learners than children.

7.3.3 *Language processing*

Language processing provides another example of an area where there may be interesting modular interactions which might differ in L1 and L2 acquisition. Processing can be divided into two separate components: comprehension and production, both of which are involved in all language use, not just in language acquisition. The language comprehension system takes linguistic input (i.e., the utterances of other speakers) and assigns a syntactic structure to it; this is technically known as parsing. The language production system allows speakers to build utterances which convey whatever they want to convey.

Bialystok and Sharwood Smith (1985) distinguish between knowledge (in our terms *competence*, consisting of UG and a language specific grammar) and control of that knowledge (i.e. the comprehension and production mechanisms that are involved in language use). They point out that IL performance will reflect both knowledge and control, and that it is possible that L2 learners who have attained a relatively sophisticated degree of L2 knowledge may nevertheless have difficulties with L2 control, so that certain L2 acquisition problems may reflect lack of control rather than lack of competence. Differences between fluency and accuracy in second language acquisition may reflect such a distinction: accuracy relates to competence but fluency is a matter of control. L2 learners can be accurate but not fluent or fluent but not accurate because competence and control of competence are actually independent of each other. Sharwood Smith (1986) suggests that the different results from imitation and comprehension tasks reported by Flynn (1987b) may reflect some such distinction. Her comprehension results suggest that subjects do in fact have good understanding of the anaphora possibilities in the L2, that they are already within their competence. The imitation results suggest that they have not, however, got full control over L2 production mechanisms. This dissociation of competence and control is another difference between L1 and L2 acquisition. In L1 acquisition, the acquisition of competence and control of competence seem to be closely connected, although the generally held view that comprehension precedes production may in fact be a case of competence preceding control of competence.

It is interesting to speculate on the possible implications of the distinction between competence and processing. For example, supposing it to be the case that L2 acquisition involves building up a new grammar for the L2, then L2 learners clearly have two different knowledge systems, one for the mother tongue and one for the L2. But what about the parsing and production systems? Do L2 learners use the same systems for processing the L2 as they do for the L1, or must new mechanisms be constructed? How can one tell? It is only with relatively sophisticated processing theories that one will be able to translate these speculations into specific claims. The fact that theories of grammar and theories of parsing are both reasonably well-developed suggests that this should be a fruitful area to extend to the second language acquisition context.

7.3.4 *Pragmatics/discourse*

Considerations beyond sentence grammar affect the way speakers choose
to express themselves, or the interpretations that hearers impose on utterances. Pragmatic or discourse factors determine which out of a range of
possible structures allowed by the grammar of a language is actually
realized in a particular context, or which out of a range of possible interpretations is assigned to a particular syntactic structure. Pragmatic knowledge
presumably draws on many different domains, including knowledge and
beliefs, and thus may be thought of as being within the central processors
rather than in the language module itself. The relationship between grammatical competence and pragmatics may be different in L1 and L2 acquisition. Rutherford (1989) and Zobl (1989) both argue that while L2 learners show considerable sensitivity to abstract properties of the L2 syntax,
their pragmatic knowledge causes them problems. In particular, learners
assume that the grammar and pragmatic factors interact in the same way in
the L1 and the L2, even when this is not the case.

7.3.5 *Communicative competence*

In second language acquisition research and in second language teaching,
competence is often defined much more broadly than the kind of linguistic
competence that has been discussed in this book. In particular, it is often
considered desirable to account for communicative competence (Hymes
1972; Canale and Swain 1980), which includes not only linguistic knowledge, but also other kinds of knowledge that may influence one's language
behaviour, whether as a language learner or native speaker.
    Considered in the light of the modularity hypothesis, it is clear that
communicative competence will draw on a variety of domains: the language
module, the central processors, and possibly other cognitive modules. In
addition, theories that look at how linguistic competence is actually used
(i.e., theories of linguistic performance) are likely to be crucially involved.
Thus, our understanding of communicative competence will ultimately
depend on a variety of theories. In pursuing the implications of UG-based
research in L2 acquisition, we have not considered many aspects of second
language knowledge and performance. The theory of UG attempts to
explain how language can be acquired and to characterize linguistic competence in the narrower sense. Understanding competence in this sense will

ultimately contribute to our understanding of competence in the broader sense as well.

7.4 Theory to practice

The research reported on here has addressed the question of whether UG is still accessible in L2 acquisition. As we have seen, the answer appears to be a qualified *yes*. One might ask whether this finding has any direct applications to language teaching. This is an area where extreme caution is needed. The aim of second language acquisition research, including UG-based research, is to reach an understanding of how languages are learned. Even when such understanding is attained, this does not necessarily offer clear insights into the best way to teach languages.

However, a couple of general observations are in order. Principles of UG, such as Subjacency, the ECP, and the Theta Criterion, are highly abstract and complex, as we have seen. It is obvious that these are not the kinds of properties of language that language teachers currently teach; they are simply not aware of them. It seems equally obvious that one should not attempt to teach this kind of knowledge. Part of the UG claim is that such properties cannot be learned; hence, presumably, it is pointless to teach them. Indeed, without realizing it, language teachers presuppose this kind of knowledge in their students; language teaching (where it is oriented towards language structure) concentrates on language particular properties rather than universal principles.

An area where UG-based research does offer potential implications for language teaching is over the question of what kind of evidence can be used to reset parameters. It is possible that specific grammar teaching and correction in the language classroom can sometimes fill a gap not covered by positive evidence from the L2. For example, Spanish learners of English may need to be told that English does not allow empty subjects, French learners of English may need to be told that English does not allow adverbs to intervene between verb and object, Japanese learners of English may need to be told that English reflexives always require a local antecedent. Even here, caution is necessary. These surface properties of English stem from deeper principles and parameters, and we do not yet know whether pointing out the surface properties of the L2 has any lasting effects on the ILG.

7.5 Conclusion: linguistic theory and L2 acquisition research

Linguistic theory is constantly developing and being revised. As we have seen, this has led to a number of problems for researchers trying to investigate the role of UG in L2 acquisition. For example, changes in theoretical assumptions about the levels of operation of principles of UG affect predictions for the operation of these principles in L2 acquisition. Changes in parameter theory lead to problems in identifying parameters and their presumed effects.

Although sometimes frustrating to the researcher who wishes to pursue the implications of UG in domains outside linguistic theory itself, in fact the benefits of working from such a theory outweigh the disadvantages. At the very least, theories like GB theory provide a highly sophisticated tool for describing and investigating the language of L2 learners. Secondly, theory development is inevitable in any area and is a sign of growth. Growth in linguistic theory offers potential insights into various domains, including second language acquisition, and it is also possible that the study of L2 acquisition may contribute to this growth. Refinements in linguistic theory lead to refinements in the way L2 acquisition is viewed, and increase our understanding of the knowledge that L2 learners attain. Thirdly, alternative theories, such as the proposal that L2 acquisition involves problem-solving (Bley-Vroman 1989) or takes place by means of general learning strategies (Clahsen and Muysken 1986), are at present very underdeveloped and lack equivalent richness, so that it is not yet possible to derive precise and testable hypotheses to test on L2 learners. Finally, despite changes in detail, the overall concept of a theory of linguistic competence, with both an innate, universal component, and a learned, language-specific grammar, remains. If we are interested in understanding what it means to attain linguistic competence in a second language, then it is crucial to have a theory of linguistic competence to provide a general frame of reference. This is true regardless of the question of whether L2 learners have access to UG; even if it turns out that L2 learners do not have the complex knowledge that would be expected under the UG hypothesis, this is something that can only be determined by investigating universal principles and parameters as they are isolated by linguists.

7.6 Further reading

i.   The implications of the modularity hypothesis for L2 acquisition are discussed in greater detail in *Sharwood Smith* (to appear), and *Schwartz* (1986, 1987). *Gregg* (1988a) provides a critique of Schwartz.

ii.   Parsing from the perspective of generative grammar is investigated by (among others) *Berwick and Weinberg* (1984), *Marcus* (1980), papers in *Dowty, Karttunen and Zwicky* (1985), papers in *Garfield* (1987).

iii.   On the possible interface between UG-based research and language teaching, see *Rutherford* (1987), *Rutherford and Sharwood Smith* (1985), *White* (in press).

References

Adjémian, C. 1976. On the nature of interlanguage systems. *Language Learning* 26: 297-320.

Adjémian, C. and J. Liceras. 1984. Accounting for adult acquisition of relative clauses: Universal Grammar, L1 and structuring the intake. In: F. Eckman, L. Bell, and D. Nelson (eds), *Universals of second language acquisition*. Rowley, MA: Newbury House.

Atkinson, M. 1982. *Explanation in the study of child language development*. Cambridge; Cambridge University Press.

Baker, C. L. 1979a. Remarks on complementizers, filters and learnability. Unpublished manuscript: University of Texas, Austin.

Baker, C. L. 1979b. Syntactic theory and the projection problem. *Linguistic Inquiry* 10: 533-581.

Baltin, M. 1981. Strict bounding. In: C.L. Baker and J. McCarthy (eds), *The logical problem of language acquisition*. Cambridge, MA: MIT Press.

Bardovi-Harlig, K. 1986. Markedness and salience in second-language acquisition. *Language Learning* 37: 385-407.

Bates, E. and B. MacWhinney. 1987. Competition, variation and language learning. In: B. MacWhinney (ed.), *Mechanisms of language acquisition*. Hillsdale, NJ: Lawrence Erlbaum.

Berwick, R. 1985. *The acquisition of syntactic knowledge*. Cambridge, MA: MIT Press.

Berwick, R. and A. Weinberg. 1984. *The grammatical basis of linguistic performance: language use and acquisition*. Cambridge, MA: MIT Press.

Bialystok, E. and M. Sharwood Smith. 1985. Interlanguage is not a state of mind: an evaluation of the construct for second language acquisition. *Applied Linguistics* 6: 101-117.

Birdsong, D. 1989. *Metalinguistic performance and interlanguage competence*. New York: Springer.

Bley-Vroman, R. 1986. Hypothesis testing in second-language acquisition theory. *Language Learning* 36: 353-376.

Bley-Vroman, R. 1989. The logical problem of second language learning. In S. Gass and J. Schachter (eds), *Linguistic perspectives on second language acquisition*. Cambridge: Cambridge University Press.

Bley-Vroman, R. and C. Chaudron. 1988. Review essay: a critique of Flynn's parameter-setting model of second language acquisition. In: C. Sato (ed.), *University of Hawai'i Working Papers in English as a Second Language* 7.1 : 67-107.

Bley-Vroman, R., S. Felix and G. Ioup. 1988. The accessibility of Universal Grammar in adult language learning. *Second Language Research* 4: 1-32.

Bohannon, J. N. and L. Stanowicz. 1988. The issue of negative evidence: adult responses to children's language errors. *Developmental Psychology* 24: 684-689.

Borer, H. and K. Wexler. 1987. The maturation of syntax. In: T. Roeper and E. Williams (eds), *Parameter setting*. Dordrecht: Reidel.

Bowerman, M. 1987. Commentary: Mechanisms of language acquisition. In: B. MacWhinney (ed.), *Mechanisms of language acquisition*. Hillsdale, NJ: Lawrence Erlbaum.

Braine, M. 1971. On two types of models of the internalization of grammars. In: D. Slobin (ed.), *The ontogenesis of grammar*. New York: Academic Press.

Brown, R. 1973. *A first language: the early stages*. Cambridge, MA: Harvard University Press.

Brown, R. 1977. Introduction. In: C. Snow and C. Ferguson (eds), *Talking to children: language input and acquisition*. Cambridge: Cambridge University Press.

Brown, R. and C. Hanlon. 1970. Derivational complexity and the order of acquisition in child speech. In: J.R. Hayes (ed.), *Cognition and the development of language*. New York: Wiley.

Burzio, L. 1981. *Intransitive verbs and Italian auxiliaries*. Unpublished doctoral dissertation, Massachusetts Institute of Technology, Cambridge MA.

Canale, M. and M. Swain. 1980. Theoretical bases of communicative approaches to second language teaching and testing. *Applied Linguistics* 1: 1-47.

Chomsky, N. 1975. *Reflections on language*. New York: Pantheon.

Chomsky, N. 1980. *Rules and representations*. Oxford: Basil Blackwell.

Chomsky, N. 1981a. *Lectures on government and binding*. Dordrecht: Foris.

Chomsky, N. 1981b. Principles and parameters in syntactic theory. In: N. Hornstein and D. Lightfoot (eds), *Explanation in linguistics: the logical problem of language acquisition*. London: Longman.

Chomsky, N. 1986. *Knowledge of language: its nature, origin, and use*. New York; Praeger.

Chomsky, N. and H. Lasnik. 1977. Filters and control. *Linguistic Inquiry* 8: 425-504.

Clahsen, H. 1984. The acquisition of German word order: a test case for cognitive approaches to L2 development. In: R. Andersen (ed.), *Second languages: a cross linguistic perspective*. Rowley, MA: Newbury House.

Clahsen, H. 1988. Parameterized grammatical theory and language acquisition: a study of the acquisition of verb placement and inflection by children and adults. In: S. Flynn, and W. O'Neil (eds), *Linguistic theory in second language acquisition*. Dordrecht: Kluwer.

Clahsen, H. and P. Muysken. 1986. The availability of Universal Grammar to adult and child learners: a study of the acquisition of German word order. *Second Language Research* 2: 93-119.

Clahsen, H. and P. Muysken. 1989. The UG paradox in L2 acquisition. *Second Language Research* 5:1-29.

Clark, E. 1987. The principle of contrast: a constraint on language acquisition. In: B. MacWhinney (ed.), *Mechanisms of language acquisition*. Hillsdale, NJ: Lawrence Erlbaum.

Comrie, B. 1981. *Language universals and linguistic typology*. Oxford: Basil Blackwell.

Cook, V. 1985. Chomsky's Universal Grammar and second language learning. *Applied Linguistics* 6: 2-18.

Cook, V. 1988. *Chomsky's Universal Grammar*. Oxford: Basil Blackwell.

Coppieters, R. 1987. Competence differences between native and near-native speakers. *Language* 63: 544-573.

Corder, S. P. 1967. The significance of learners' errors. *International Review of Applied Linguistics in Language Teaching* 5: 161-170.

Corder, S. P. 1978. Language distance and the magnitude of the language learning task. *Studies in Second Language Acquisition* 2: 27-36.

Crain, S. and J.D. Fodor. In press. Competence and performance in child language. In E. Dromi (ed.), *Language and cognition; a developmental perspective*. Norwood, NJ: Ablex.

Crain, S. and C. McKee. 1986. Acquisition of structural restrictions on anaphora. In: *Proceedings of the North Eastern Linguistic Society 16*. University of Massachusetts at Amherst: Graduate Linguistics Students Association.

Dowty, D., L. Karttunen and A. Zwicky (eds). 1985. *Natural language processing*. Cambridge: Cambridge University Press.

du Plessis, J., D. Solin, L. Travis and L. White. 1987. UG or not UG, that is the question: a reply to Clahsen and Muysken. *Second Language Research* 3: 56-75.

Dulay, H. and M. Burt. 1974a. Natural sequences in child second language acquisition. *Language Learning* 24: 37-53.

Dulay, H. and M. Burt. 1974b. A new perspective on the creative construction processes in child second language acquisition. *Language Learning* 24: 253-258 .

Eckman, F. 1977. Markedness and the contrastive analysis hypothesis. *Language Learning* 27: 315-330.

Ellis, R. 1986. *Understanding second language acquisition*. Oxford: Oxford University Press.

Eubank, L. 1989. Parameters and L2 learning: Flynn revisited. *Second Language Research* 5: 43-73.

Felix, S. 1984. Maturational aspects of universal grammar. In: A. Davies, C. Criper and A. Howatt (eds), *Interlanguage*. Edinburgh: Edinburgh University Press.

Felix, S. 1985. More evidence on competing cognitive systems. *Second Language Research* 1: 47-72.

Felix, S. 1988. UG-generated knowledge in adult second language acquisition. In: S. Flynn and W. O'Neil (eds), *Linguistic theory in second language acquisition*. Dordrecht: Kluwer.

Finer, D. and E. Broselow. 1986. Second language acquisition of reflexive-binding. In: *Proceedings of the North Eastern Linguistic Society 16*. University of Massachusetts at Amherst: Graduate Linguistics Students Association.

Finer, D. 1989. Binding parameters in second language acquisition. Paper presented at the Second Language Research Forum, UCLA, Los Angeles, Feb.1989. To appear in L. Eubank (ed.), *Point/counterpoint*.

Flynn, S. 1984. A universal in L2 acquisition based on a PBD typology. In: F. Eckman, L. Bell and D. Nelson (eds), *Universals of second language acquisition*. Rowley, MA: Newbury House.

Flynn, S. 1987a. Contrast and construction in a parameter-setting model of L2 acquisition. *Language Learning* 37: 19-62.

Flynn, S. 1987b. *A parameter-setting model of L2 acquisition*. Dordrecht: Reidel.

Flynn, S. 1987c. Second language acquisition of pronoun anaphora:resetting the parameter. In: B. Lust (ed.), *Studies in the acquisition of anaphora, Vol.11: applying the constraints*. Dordrecht: Reidel.

Flynn, S. and W. O'Neil (eds). 1988. *Linguistic theory in second language acquisition*. Dordrecht: Kluwer.

Fodor, J.A. 1983. *The modularity of mind*. Cambridge, MA: MIT Press.

Fodor, J.D. and S. Crain. 1987. Simplicity and generality of rules in language acquisition. In: B. MacWhinney (ed.), *Mechanisms of language acquisition*. Hillsdale, NJ: Lawrence Erbaum.

French, M. 1985. Markedness and the acquisition of pied-piping and preposition stranding. *McGill Working Papers in Linguistics* 2.1: 131-144.

Garfield, J. (ed.). 1987. *Modularity in knowledge representation and natural language understanding*. Cambridge, MA: MIT Press.

Gass, S. 1979. Language transfer and universal grammatical relations. *Language Learning* 29: 327-344.

Gass, S. and J. Schachter (eds). 1989. *Linguistic perspectives on second language acquisition*. Cambridge: Cambridge University Press.

Goodluck, H. 1986. Language acquisition and linguistic theory. In: P. Fletcher and M. Garman (eds), *Language acquisition (2nd edition)*. Cambridge: Cambridge University Press.

Goodluck, H. 1987. Children's interpretation of pronouns and null NPs: an alternative view. In: B. Lust (ed.), *Studies in the acquisition of anaphora, Vol.11: applying the constraints*. Dordrecht: Reidel.

Goodluck, H. In press. *Language acquisition: a linguistic introduction*. Oxford: Basil Blackwell.

Greenberg, J. 1966. Some universals of grammar with particular reference to the order of meaningful elements. In: J. Greenberg (ed.), *Universals of language*. Cambridge, MA: MIT Press.

Gregg, K. 1988a. Epistemology without knowledge: Schwartz on Chomsky, Fodor and Krashen. *Second Language Research* 4: 66-80.

Gregg, K. 1988b. The variable competence model of second language acquisition, and why it isn't. To appear in *Applied Linguistics*.

Gregg, K. 1989. Second language acquisition theory: the case for a generative perspective. In: S. Gass and J. Schachter (eds), *Linguistic perspectives on second language acquisition*. Cambridge: Cambridge University Press.

Grimshaw, J. and S.T. Rosen. In press. Knowledge and obedience: the developmental status of the Binding Theory. *Linguistic Inquiry* 21.2

Hale, K. 1983. Warlpiri and the grammar of non-configurational languages. *Natural Language and Linguistic Theory* 1: 1-43.

Hawkins, J. 1987. Implicational universals as predictors of language acquisition. *Linguistics* 25: 453-473.

Hildebrand, J. 1987. The acquisition of preposition stranding. *Canadian Journal of Linguistics* 32.1: 65-85.

Hilles, S. 1986. Interlanguage and the pro-drop parameter. *Second Language Research* 2: 33-52.

Hirakawa, M. 1989. L2 acquisition of English reflexives by speakers of Japanese. Paper presented at the Conference on the interaction of linguistics, second language acquisition and speech pathology, University of Wisconsin-Milwaukee, April 1989.

Hirsh-Pasek, K., R. Treiman and M. Schneiderman. 1984. Brown and Hanlon revisited: mothers' sensitivity to ungrammatical forms. *Journal of Child Language* 11: 81-88.

Huang, C. J. 1982. *Logical relations in Chinese and the theory of grammar*. Unpublished doctoral dissertation: Massachusetts Institute of Technology, Cambridge MA.

Hyams, N. 1986. *Language acquisition and the theory of parameters*. Dordrecht: Reidel.

Hyltenstam, K. 1984. The use of typological markedness conditions as predictors in second language acquisition: the case of pronominal copies in relative clauses. In: R. Andersen (ed.), *Second languages: a cross-linguistic perspective*. Rowley, MA: Newbury House.

Hymes, D. 1972. On communicative competence. In J.B. Pride and J. Holmes (eds), *Sociolinguistics*. Harmondsworth: Penguin.

Jaeggli, O. 1982. *Topics in Romance syntax*. Dordrecht: Foris.

Jaeggli, O. and N. Hyams. 1988. Morphological uniformity and the setting of the null subject parameter. In: *Proceedings of the North Eastern Linguistic Society 18*, University of Massachusetts at Amherst: Graduate Linguistics Students Association.

Jaeggli, O. and K. Safir. 1989. The null subject parameter and parametric theory. In: O. Jaeggli and K. Safir (eds), *The null subject parameter*. Dordrecht: Kluwer.

Johnson, J. and E. Newport. 1989. Critical period effects in second language learning: the influence of maturational state on the acquisition of English as a second language. *Cognitive Psychology* 21: 60-99.

Kean, M. 1986. Core issues in transfer. In: E. Kellerman and M. Sharwood Smith (eds), *Cross linguistic influence in second language acquisition*. Oxford: Pergamon.

Kellerman, E. 1979. Transfer and non-transfer: where are we now? *Studies in Second Language Acquisition* 2.1: 37-57.

Kellerman, E. 1983. Now you see it, now you don't. In: S. Gass and L. Selinker (eds), *Language transfer in language learning*. Rowley, MA: Newbury House.

Kellerman, E. 1985. Dative alternation and the analysis of data: a reply to Mazurkewich. *Language Learning* 35: 91-106.

Kleinmann, H. 1978. The strategy of avoidance in adult second language acquisition. *Language Learning* 27: 93-107.

Koopman, H. 1984. *The syntax of verbs*. Dordrecht: Foris.

Krashen, S. 1981. *Second language acquisition and second language learning*. Oxford: Pergamon Press.

Krause, M. and H. Goodluck. 1983. Children's interpretations of wh-question constructions. In: Y. Otsu, H. Van Riemsdijk, K. Inoue, A. Kamio and N. Kawasaki (eds), *Studies in generative grammar and language acquisition*. Tokyo: International Christian University.

Kuno, S. 1973. *The structure of the Japanese language*. Cambridge, MA: MIT Press.

Labov, W. 1972. *Sociolinguistic patterns*. Philadelphia: University of Pennsylvania Press.

Lasnik, H. and S. Crain. 1985. Review article: On the acquisition of pronominal reference. *Lingua* 65: 135-154.

Lasnik, H. and J. Uriagereka. 1988. *A course in GB syntax: lectures on binding and empty categories*. Cambridge, MA: MIT Press.

Liceras, J. 1985. The role of intake in the determination of learners' competence. In: S. Gass and C. Madden (eds), *Input in second language acquisition*. Rowley, MA: Newbury House.

Liceras, J. 1986. *Linguistic theory and second language acquisition*. Tübingen: Narr.

Liceras, J. 1988a. L2 learnability: delimiting the domain of core grammar as distinct from the marked periphery. In: S. Flynn and W. O'Neil (eds), *Linguistic theory in second language acquisition*. Dordrecht: Kluwer.

Liceras, J. 1988b. Syntax and stylistics: more on the pro-drop parameter. In: J. Pankhurst, M. Sharwood Smith and P. Van Buren (eds), *Learnability and second languages: a book of readings*. Dordrecht: Foris.

Lightbown, P. M. and L. White. 1988. The influence of linguistic theories on language acquisition research: description and explanation. *Language Learning* 37: 483-510.

Lightfoot, D. 1982. *The language lottery: toward a biology of grammars*. Cambridge, MA: MIT Press.

Long, M. 1988. Maturational constraints on language development. In: C. Sato (ed.), *University of Hawai'i Working Papers in English as a Second Language* 7.1: 1-54.

Lust, B. 1981. Constraints on anaphora in child language: a prediction for a universal. In: S. Tavakolian (ed.), *Language acquisition and linguistic theory*. Cambridge, MA: MIT Press.

Lust, B. 1983. On the notion 'principle branching direction': a parameter of Universal Grammar. In: Y. Otsu, H. Van Riemsdijk, K. Inoue, A. Kamio and N. Kawasaki (eds), *Studies in generative grammar and language acquisition*. Tokyo: International Christian University.

Lust, B. (ed.). 1986. *Studies in the acquisition of anaphora, Vol I: defining the constraints*. Dordrecht: Reidel.

Lust, B. (ed.). 1987. *Studies in the acquisition of anaphora, Vol.11: applying the constraints*. Dordrecht: Reidel.

Manzini, R. and K. Wexler. 1987. Parameters, binding theory, and learnability. *Linguistic Inquiry* 18: 413-444.

Marcus, M. 1980. *A theory of syntactic recognition for natural language*. Cambridge, MA: MIT Press.

Martohardjono, G. and J. Gair. 1989. Apparent UG inaccessibility in SLA: misapplied principles or principled misapplications? Paper presented at the Conference on the interaction of linguistics, second language acquisition and speech pathology, University of Wisconsin-Milwaukee, April 1989.

Mazurkewich, I. 1984a. The acquisition of the dative alternation by second language learners and linguistic theory. *Language Learning* 34: 91-109.

Mazurkewich, I. 1984b. Dative questions and markedness. In: F. Eckman, L. Bell and D. Nelson (eds), *Universals of second language acquisition*. Rowley, MA: Newbury House.

Mazurkewich, I. 1988. The acquisition of infinitive and gerund complements by second language learners. In: S. Flynn and W. O'Neil (eds), *Linguistic theory in second language acquisition*. Dordrecht: Kluwer.

McLaughlin, B. 1987. *Theories of second language learning*. London: Edward Arnold.

Newmeyer, F. 1983. *Grammatical theory: its limits and its possibilities*. Chicago: University of Chicago Press.

O'Grady, W. 1987. *Principles of grammar and learning*. Chicago: Chicago University Press.

O'Grady, W., Y. Suzuki-Wei and W.C. Sook. 1986. Directionality preferences in the interpretation of anaphora: data from Korean and Japanese. *Journal of Child Language* 13: 409-420.

Otsu, Y. 1981. *Universal grammar and syntactic development in children: toward a theory of syntactic development*. Unpublished doctoral dissertation: Massachusetts Institute of Technology, Cambridge MA.

Otsu, Y. and K. Naoi. 1986. Structure-dependence in L2 acquisition. Paper presented at J.A.C.E.T., Keio University, Tokyo, Sept. 1986.

Pankhurst, J., M. Sharwood Smith and P. Van Buren (eds). 1988. *Learnability and second languages: a book of readings*. Dordrecht: Foris.

Phinney, M. 1981. *Syntactic constraints and the acquisition of embedded sentential complements*. Unpublished doctoral dissertation: University of Massachusetts, Amherst.

Phinney, M. 1987. The pro-drop parameter in second language acquisition. In: T. Roeper and E. Williams (eds), *Parameter setting*. Dordrecht: Reidel.

Pinker, S. 1984. *Language learnability and language development*. Cambridge, MA: Harvard University Press.

Pollock, J. 1989. Verb movement, UG and the structure of IP. *Linguistic Inquiry* 20: 365-424.

Radford, A. 1981. *Transformational syntax: a student's guide to Chomsky's extended standard theory*. Cambridge: Cambridge University Press.

Radford, A. 1988. *Transformational grammar: a first course*. Cambridge: Cambridge University Press.

Reinhart, T. 1986. Center and periphery in the grammar of anaphora. In: B. Lust (ed.), *Studies in the acquisition of anaphora, Vol I: defining the constraints*. Dordrecht: Reidel.

Ritchie, W. 1978. The right roof constraint in adult-acquired language. In: W. Ritchie (ed.), *Second language acquisition research: issues and implications*. New York: Academic Press.

Ritchie, W. 1983. Universal grammar and second language acquisition. In: D. Rogers and J. Sloboda (eds), *The acquisition of symbolic skills*. New York: Plenum Press.

Rizzi, L. 1982. *Issues in Italian syntax*. Dordrecht: Foris.

Rizzi, L. 1986. Null objects in Italian and the theory of *pro*. *Linguistic Inquiry* 17: 501-557.

Roeper, T. and E. Williams (eds). 1987. *Parameter setting*. Dordrecht: Reidel.

Ross, J. 1967. *Constraints on variables in syntax*. Unpublished doctoral dissertation: Massachusetts Institute of Technology, Cambridge MA.

Rutherford, W. 1983. Language typology and language transfer. In: S. Gass and L. Selinker (eds), *Language transfer in language learning*. Rowley, MA: Newbury House.

Rutherford, W. 1987. *Second language grammar: learning and teaching*. London: Longman.

Rutherford, W. 1988. Questions of learnability in second language acquisition. Paper presented at the Boston University Conference on Language Development, Boston, Oct.1988.

Rutherford, W. 1989. Interlanguage and pragmatic word-order. In: S. Gass and J. Schachter (eds), *Linguistic perspectives on second language acquisition*. Cambridge: Cambridge University Press.

Rutherford, W. and M. Sharwood Smith. 1985. Consciousness-raising and Universal Grammar. *Applied Linguistics* 6: 274-282.

Saito, M. 1985. *Some assymetries in Japanese and their theoretical implications*. Unpublished doctoral dissertation: Massachusetts Institute of Technology, Cambridge MA.

Schachter, J. 1974. An error in error analysis. *Language Learning* 26: 205-214.

Schachter, J. 1988a. On the issue of completeness in second language acquisition. Paper presented at the Boston University Conference on Language Development, Boston, Oct.1988.

Schachter, J. 1988b. Second language acquisition and its relationship to Universal Grammar. *Applied Linguistics* 9: 219-235.

Schachter, J. 1989a. A new look at an old classic. *Second Language Research* 5: 30-42.

Schachter, J. 1989b. Testing a proposed universal. In: S. Gass and J. Schachter (eds), *Linguistic perspectives on second language acquisition*. Cambridge: Cambridge University Press.

Schumann, J. 1978. *The pidginization process*. Rowley, MA: Newbury House.

Schwartz, B. 1986. The epistemological status of second language acquisition. *Second Language Research* 2: 120-159.

Schwartz, B. 1987. *The modular basis of second language acquisition*. Unpublished doctoral dissertation: University of Southern California, Los Angeles.

Schwartz, B. and A. Tomaselli. 1988. Some implications from an analysis of German word order. Paper presented at the Fifth Workshop on Comparative Germanic Syntax, Groningen, 1988.

Selinker, L. 1972. Interlanguage. *International Review of Applied Linguistics in Language Teaching* 10: 209-231.

Sells, P. 1985. *Lectures on contemporary syntactic theories*. Stanford, CA: Center for the Study of Language and Information.

Sharwood Smith, M. 1986. The competence/control model applied to cross-linguistic influence in the creation of new grammars. In: E. Kellerman and M. Sharwood Smith (eds), *Cross-linguistic influence in second language acquisition*. Oxford: Pergamon.

Sharwood Smith, M. To appear. *Interlanguage*.

Slobin, D. 1973. Cognitive prerequisites for the development of grammar. In: C. Ferguson and D. Slobin (eds), *Studies of child language development*. New York: Holt, Rinehart and Winston.

Slobin, D. (ed.). 1986. *The cross linguistic study of language acquisition*. Vols. 1 and 2. Hillsdale, NJ: Lawrence Erlbaum.

Slobin, D. and T. Bever. 1982. Children use canonical sentence schemas: a cross-linguistic study of word order and inflections. *Cognition* 12: 229-265.

Smith, N. and D. Wilson. 1979. *Modern linguistics: the results of Chomsky's revolution*. Harmondsworth: Penguin.

Snow, C. and C. Ferguson (eds). 1977. *Talking to children: language input and acquisition*. Cambridge: Cambridge University Press.

Solan, L. 1983. *Pronominal reference: child language and the theory of grammar*. Dordrecht: Reidel.

Sportiche, D. 1981. Bounding nodes in French. *Linguistic Review* 1: 219-246.

Stowell, T. 1981. *Origins of phrase-structure*. Unpublished doctoral dissertation: Massachusetts Institute of Technology, Cambridge MA.

Tarone, E. 1988. *Variation in interlanguage*. London: Edward Arnold.

Tavakolian, S. (ed.). 1981. *Language acquisition and linguistic theory*. Cambridge, MA: MIT Press.

Thiersch, C. 1978. *Topics in German syntax*. Unpublished doctoral dissertation: Massachusetts Institute of Technology, Cambridge MA.

Thomas, M. 1989. The interpretation of English reflexive pronouns by non-native speakers. *Studies in Second Language Acquisition* 11: 281-303.

Travis, L. 1984. *Parameters and effects of word order variation*. Unpublished doctoral dissertation: Massachusetts Institute of Technology, Cambridge MA.

Van Buren, P. and M. Sharwood. 1985. The acquisition of preposition stranding by second language learners and parametric variation. *Second Language Research* 1: 18-26.

Van Riemsdijk, H. and E. Williams. 1986. *Introduction to the theory of grammar*. Cambridge, MA: MIT Press.

Wexler, K. 1981. Some issues in the theory of learnability. In: C.L. Baker and J. McCarthy (eds), *The logical problem of language acquisition*. Cambridge, MA: MIT Press.

Wexler, K. and P. Culicover. 1980. *Formal principles of language acquisition*. Cambridge, MA: MIT Press.

Wexler, K. and R. Manzini. 1987. Parameters and learnability in binding theory. In: T. Roeper and E. Williams (eds), *Parameter setting*. Dordrecht: Reidel.

White, L. 1982. *Grammatical theory and language acquisition*. Dordrecht: Foris.

White, L. 1985a. The acquisition of parameterized grammars: subjacency in second language acquisition. *Second Language Research* 1: 1-17.

White, L. 1985b. Is there a logical problem of second language acquisition? *TESL Canada* 2.2: 29-41.

White, L. 1985c. The pro-drop parameter in adult second language acquisition. *Language Learning* 35: 47-62.

White, L. 1986a. Implications of parametric variation for adult second language acquisition: an investigation of the 'pro-drop' parameter. In: V. Cook (ed.), *Experimental approaches to second language acquisition*. Oxford: Pergamon.

White, L. 1986b. Markedness and parameter setting: some implications for a theory of adult second language acquisition. In: F. Eckman, E. Moravscik and J. Wirth (eds), *Markedness*. New York: Plenum Press.

White, L. 1987a. Against comprehensible input: the input hypothesis and the development of L2 competence. *Applied Linguistics* 8: 95-110.

White, L. 1987b. Markedness and second language acquisition: the question of transfer. *Studies in Second Language Acquisition* 9: 261-286.

White, L. 1987c. Universal Grammar: Is it just a new name for old problems? Paper presented at Second Language Research Forum, USC, Los Angeles, Feb.1987.

White, L. 1988a. Island effects in second language acquisition. In: S. Flynn and W. O'Neil (eds), *Linguistic theory in second language acquisition*. Dordrecht: Kluwer.

White, L. 1988b. Universal Grammar and language transfer. In: J. Pankhurst, M. Sharwood Smith and P. Van Buren, P. (eds), *Learnability and second languages: a book of readings*. Dordrecht: Foris.

White, L. 1989a. The principle of adjacency in second language acquisition: do L2 learners observe the subset principle? In: S. Gass and J. Schachter (eds), *Linguistic perspectives on second language acquisition*. Cambridge: Cambridge University Press.

White, L. 1989b. Processing strategies: are they sufficient for explaining adult SLA? Paper presented at the Second Language Research Forum, UCLA, Los Angeles, Feb.1989. To appear in L. Eubank (ed.), *Point/counterpoint*.

White, L. 1989c. The verb-movement parameter in second language acquisition: some effects of positive and negative evidence in the classroom. Paper presented at the Boston University Conference on Language Development, Boston, Oct. 1989.

White, L. To appear. Argument structure in second language acquisition. In: H. Nicholas (ed.), *Explaining interlanguage development*.

White, L. In press. Implications of learnability theories for second language learning and teaching. In: M.A.K. Halliday, J. Gibbons and H. Nicholas (eds), *Learning, keeping and using language*. Amsterdam: John Benjamins.

Zobl, H. 1983. Markedness and the projection problem. *Language Learning* 33: 293-313.

Zobl, H. 1988. Configurationality and the subset principle: the acquisition of V' by Japanese learners of English. In: J. Pankhurst, M. Sharwood Smith and P. Van Buren (eds), *Learnability and second languages: a book of readings*. Dordrecht: Foris.

Zobl, H. 1989. Modularity in adult L2 acquisition. *Language Learning* 39.

Appendix: Abbreviations used in the book

BA = backwards anaphora
COMP = complementizer
ECP = Empty Category Principle
ESL = English as a second language
FA = forwards anaphora
GB = Government and Binding
GCP = Governing Category Parameter
GJ = grammaticality judgment
IL = interlanguage
ILG = interlanguage grammar
INFL = inflection
LF = logical form
L1 = first language
L2 = second language
LB = left-branching
M = marked
N = noun
NP = nounphrase
PBD = Principal Branching Direction
PP = prepositional phrase
RB = right-branching
SOV = subject object verb
SVO = subject verb object
U = unmarked
UG = Universal Grammar
V = Verb
VP = verbphrase
VS = verb subject

Index